I AM DEBRA LEE

I AM DEBRA LEE

~

A MEMOIR

DEBRA LEE

FORMER CEO OF BET NETWORKS

LEGACY
LIT

NEW YORK BOSTON

Copyright © 2023 by Debra Lee

Cover design by Tree Abraham. Cover photograph by Anderson Hopkins. Cover copyright © 2023 by Hachette Book Group, Inc.

Legacy Lit, an imprint of Grand Central Publishing
Hachette Book Group
1290 Avenue of the Americas
New York, NY 10104
LegacyLitBooks.com
Twitter.com/LegacyLitBooks
Instagram.com/LegacyLitBooks

First Edition: March 2023

Grand Central Publishing is a division of Hachette Book Group, Inc. The Legacy Lit and Grand Central Publishing names and logos are trademarks of Hachette Book Group, Inc.

The publisher is not responsible for websites (or their content) that are not owned by the publisher.

The Hachette Speakers Bureau provides a wide range of authors for speaking events. To find out more, go to www.hachettespeakersbureau.com or call (866) 376-6591.

Legacy Lit books may be purchased in bulk for business, educational, or promotional use. For information, please contact your local bookseller or the Hachette Book Group Special Markets Department at special.markets@hbgusa.com.

Library of Congress Control Number: 2022947910

ISBNs: 978-0-3068-2859-1(hardcover), 978-0-3068-2861-4 (ebook)

Printed in the United States of America

LSC-C

Printing 1, 2022

To Ava, my daughter, my best friend,
and my inspiration.

To Quinn, my son. We lost you much too early.
I miss you every minute of every day.

To all the shy girls, the introverts.
Believe in yourself, work hard, use your voice,
and you can be anything you want to be.

CONTENTS

CONTENTS

I AM
DEBRA
LEE

INTRODUCTION

"What salary do you see yourself making in life?"

Wait, is he serious? For weeks I'd been contemplating that same million-dollar question. But I had no idea that my boss, BET's charismatic chairman and CEO, Bob Johnson, noticed the wheels churning in my head. Or that I had one foot already out the door. Bob was Bob though. He always knew what you were thinking before you said it—and he loved to put folks on the spot, which is exactly what he was doing by casually asking me "my number" over lunch. "What do you see yourself making in life?" My answer was simple: more. But I couldn't say that. It had been nearly a decade since Bob hired me away from Big Law to become BET's first general counsel. The open sky of the network's possibilities had drawn me in and convinced me to take a huge pay cut. Now, almost 10 years and as many jobs later, I deserved more. Bob knew that but had shot me down months before when I requested a raise. What my boss didn't know was that I had been plotting my exit ever since.

I took a beat, looked directly in his eyes, and offered my honest answer: "A million dollars."

"A million? That's it?" he said with a smirk.

I shook my head. This was just like Bob. Pulling me back in when he knew I was on my way out.

It had taken me a long time (too long) to work up the courage to ask for a much-deserved raise—nothing big, I'd requested maybe 10 percent more than what I'd been making—and Bob's "no" was practically instant. When I first joined BET in 1986, I begrudgingly accepted an $18,000 pay cut. Cable was the Wild Wild West of communications, and I wanted in after five years of trying to shoehorn myself into a white-shoe law firm. By the time BET came around I was more than ready to leap into a new adventure. Plus, Bob assured me that I'd be making much more eventually. He'd all but guaranteed that his company was going to be the next big thing in the budding cable industry and the media world at large. The man spun magic. A salesman if there ever was one, Bob could convince anyone of anything. One of his favorite pastimes was proving to anyone who'd listen that bacon wasn't pork! The man was unbelievable—and yet we all believed. His vision was the future, and the rest of us better hop on board or be left in the dust. He knew how to read people and get what he wanted. In a profile about his budding cable company, *Washingtonian Magazine* dubbed Bob "the Smooth Operator," and that title followed him throughout his career. If Bob said the money would follow, then it would. Or so I thought.

But as the years racked up, so did my responsibilities. I was quite literally doing the *most*: spearheading our IPO, developing new business strategy, overseeing the construction of our first production studio, even heading up our budding magazine division. Bob's favorite saying back then was "Oh, don't worry, Debra can do that." I could, and I did.

"Look, I'm doing all these extra jobs," I explained during a long-overdue compensation committee meeting with Bob and Tyrone Brown and Herb Wilkins, both board members of BET Holdings. "I don't mind doing the work. I love it, in fact. But we all know it's a lot and much more than what my singular title of General Counsel indicated. I think my pay should reflect that, don't you?" The two of them remained silent and took me in from across the table, revealing nothing. Bob's philosophy had always been "pay everyone the same." All the senior vice presidents earned equal salaries and identical pay increases. On the surface it seemed fair, although it was anything but. It took guts to stand up for oneself in that environment—and my stomach was in knots the entire time—but I knew what I was worth. The question was, did they?

"I'm just asking for recognition that I'm doing more and more extra work," I said.

"Debra," began Herb in a tone that was both condescending and unsurprising. "There are a ton of folks who would kill for a job like yours. If you don't like what Bob pays you, then you should probably leave." And that's exactly what I did. I excused myself from the table, power walked to the restaurant's bathroom, and cried.

This wasn't just about the money. That was never my North Star. I cried because my time at BET was over and I knew it. They'd crossed a line between what was fair and what was downright insulting. I'd spent nine years working harder and longer than what my job description called for, and they still didn't respect me. There was no way I could pour so much of myself into a company and get nothing in return but a pat on the back. I didn't want to leave, I had to.

I splashed cold water on my face and went back to my seat at the table with a tight smile. Herb looked satisfied as I eased back into my chair and silently picked at my plate. Bob knew exactly how upset I was; my eyes were still red. But we never talked about my salary again. That is until the million-dollar lunch a few months later.

"A million? That's it?" The zeros didn't matter. Listen, my mother worked as a ward clerk at the Black hospital in town, and my dad was a career military man. A million dollars was and is a lot of money. But what I didn't realize then was that I could and should dream bigger, not only for myself but for them. I was trained to be a lawyer—to close the deals that made everyone else money— and my vision for my future had yet to catch up to my potential. I could've said $10 million, $25 million. What Bob really wanted to know was how big I saw my career, not my bank account. That smirk? He wasn't mocking me (well, maybe a little), he was giving me a nudge. A million wasn't enough because this wasn't about a number, it was about where I wanted to go. Was I content being the network's general counsel forever, or did I see myself as more?

"Would you ever consider being COO, Debra?" COO? I was weeks away from handing in my resignation because the man wouldn't give me a 10 percent raise, and now he wanted to hand me the number two position?

The COO position was never on my vision board. First of all, the job didn't even exist. BET was Bob's company, and everyone there assumed he'd run it until the day he died. But his tight grip was taking its toll, and I think he knew that eventually he'd have to loosen the reins if he wanted the company to be his true legacy, lasting well beyond his tenure. And remember Bob's favorite saying: "Debra can do it." In reality, I'd been doing the job of COO for years, and still I'd never thought to ask for the official title. And, as I'd later discover, a few of my male colleagues on the senior executive team had already asked to be named COO—an opportunity I didn't even know was possible.

The situation, of course, proved that old corporate adage that men apply for promotions based on potential while women reach higher based on proof. We wait—sometimes for years, keeping our heads down and working hard until we feel confident enough in our earned skill set to move forward. That's what I'd been doing. Bob was pushing me out of my comfort zone but not off a cliff. I deserved to be number two. I just needed to see myself in the role. Shortly after that million-dollar lunch, Bob named me COO, a job I never saw myself doing and a job I would hold for the next ten years before eventually taking over for Bob as CEO. And to think I had been ready to quit.

Opportunities abound even when we can't see them. My life and career have been filled with possibilities I didn't see coming— from my childhood in Greensboro, North Carolina, to Harvard Law School and beyond. The trick is to be ready to accept the challenges when they finally reveal themselves. Don't shrink under the weight of your potential success—because it *is* heavy— but allow yourself the space to grow into it. Be patient and give yourself plenty of grace as you rack up wins and losses—you'll get there. As COO, I dove into every aspect of day-to-day management from programming to advertising to human resources. I had to get used to the men in the room—many of them Bob's pals and my former peers—chafing at the very idea of reporting to me. The learning curve was steep, and I've never been a fan of roller coasters, but I strapped myself in and went for it. The biggest hill to climb? The fact that I was allegedly too nice.

My entire life I'd been trained to be the best, but not to expect the title, the respect, and the compensation that should come with being at the top of your game. Working hard was supposed to be its own reward. My father, a major in the army, took great pride in me being "nice" and always emphasized that I be a good girl— modest, quiet, selfless—which meant doing the work, keeping my head down, and rarely speaking up for myself. That mindset stayed with me for decades. But if I was going to succeed in the male-dominated corporate world, that approach would have to change—and fast.

—

"*YSB* isn't working, Debra. Just shut it down, the whole damn operation," said Bob from his corner office. I'd been COO for exactly six months, and I had begun pinching myself, but not in a good "This is the job of my dreams, I could pinch myself!" kind of way. The pinching was a nervous tic. "It's just not working, and I'm tired of losing money," Bob barked. "Get it done."

Here we go, I thought. Bob wanted what he wanted when he wanted it. I knew this was a bad call, one that I would be forced to fix down the road, but I couldn't bring myself to contradict him. Instead of giving him a piece of my mind, I quietly slipped the hand resting on my lap underneath my thigh and pinched—hard.

But this one really hurt. *YSB*, which stood for *Young Sisters and Brothers*, had been my baby from the start. It was the first national lifestyle magazine for Black teenagers. As head of the publishing division, I oversaw a team of 60 people who for five years worked their tails off to produce a high-class glossy that was making an impact on the budding hip-hop generation. Bob once told me, "It's just 60 pages put together with a staple. Easy." That was another one of his Bobisms—"It's simple." Normally it motivated you to rise to the challenge. There was no question in his world whether you could do it—just get it done.

But publishing a monthly magazine that tackled culture, current events, and more was far from easy. It was hard work, and we had done the impossible year after year on an incredibly tight budget. Shutting *YSB* down felt like a betrayal to our mission at BET to uplift Black voices and also to the talented team I had handpicked. In the end, it was our bottom line that sealed the magazine's fate. We'd been operating at a loss for years, and Bob, like any CEO, didn't like losing money. I understood that as COO, but the failure still stung. What's more, I had never been in control of the magazine's advertising sales and didn't think the company had tried hard enough to market the title. But Bob would hear none of that. He had decided it was time, and now it was my job to do his dirty work.

Later, in the bathroom mirror, I would have all the snappy corporate comebacks, running down *YSB*'s profit margins and ROI that a little patience could earn us. But in person? My tongue was lead. Speaking up was never my superpower even as the company's number two. It would take years for me to get used to the sound of my own voice. Instead, I pinched myself. It got me through the rest of that meeting with Bob and later that same day when I had to take the elevator from the executive office suites down to the conference room on the *YSB* floor and deliver the bad news about the magazine. Causing myself pain allowed me to put things in perspective and redirect the sting of chauvinism to something more manageable in real time. *Okay, this was tough, but I was tougher.* The pain was relative. I could muscle through another meeting voiceless with just one pinch.

Eventually the bruises—both psychical and emotional—caught up with me. My silence wasn't protecting me, it was rendering me invisible. My voice, my opinions, my passions were being muted, and I was the one with my thumb on the button. It took far too long for me to recognize that what I brought to the table—a brilliant legal mind, public policy expertise, a love of Black culture, and a soft touch paired with a tough spirit— deserved some airtime. That I was in the room for a reason. Playing small and staying quiet not only stole my power, but it also took away my purpose. I couldn't let that happen. Because I did have a purpose—I always knew that. I wanted to amplify Black stories, build up the community, celebrate our culture, and usher more Black people, particularly Black women, into positions of power. Really, at the end of the day, what I wanted was for us to be seen. But first I had to see myself.

My power wasn't just being in the room, it was owning the room. Being happy to be there doesn't serve anyone or anything. I no longer sit quietly while "the experts" talk over me. I am the expert. I speak up. It took an unprecedented climb to the top ranks of corporate America to learn how, and in this book, I'll show you each and every step. I had to learn how to lead like Debra and not like my dad or Bob or anyone else. How to reconcile my personal responsibility with my passion and my power. How the revolution can happen in corporate America. How money isn't contrary to community uplift. How to have the following conversation:

"Debra, you talk too much in board meetings," he said. Did I hear this man right? I'd been on the board of this company for nearly two years, and he'd been there before I started. He called stating that he had something urgent to discuss and cut straight to the chase. I'll call him Peter.

Me? Talk too much? That's rich. "Really, Peter? Come on. You know that's not me at all."

"Well, if everyone talked as much as you do, we'd never get out of our board meetings," he chided.

The old me, the Debra who'd pinch her thighs during difficult business conversations, would have apologized. She would have shrunk to make everyone else more comfortable and to keep things moving along smoothly. She wouldn't have pushed back. But that Debra had been gone a long time now.

"Well, Peter," I began, "after George Floyd's murder, companies are talking about race in the boardroom, and I speak up when those issues are raised. I'm the only Black woman on the board, remember? And I'm the only person on the board who has certain expertise. So when people come in to discuss those areas, I ask the questions that others don't know to ask—"

"—we have other people who know something about—," he cut in.

"No, let me finish. That's not the same, and you know it. I'm an expert here, and you better believe I've got a lot to say. I won't apologize for knowing more and sharing that knowledge with the board. You're welcome."

CHAPTER ONE

FOR THE CULTURE

As a leader, the power of "yes" can be dizzying. Knowing that your thumbs-up can launch a career or create a cultural moment can make the top spot feel more like a throne. The yes is power. But, of course, it's the no that truly tests your ability to lead. Because for every green light there are five times as many reds—and roadblocks. One yes is only possible because of all the noes you had to navigate to get there. And despite all the practice you get—and, believe me, you'll get a lot—saying no is one of the toughest parts of the job. Nobody wants to hear it. Musical giants, rap moguls, corporate executives, and record label heads? Even less so. But whether you're running a 24-hour cable network or a two-person team at a boutique company, getting cozy and comfortable with saying no is the real superpower. Just ask

Aretha Franklin, the woman who taught me to say it, mean it, and respect it.

What's funny is that I could never figure out if Aretha liked me.

Okay, let's back up a bit. The first thing you must know is that I don't just love Black culture—the magic in our hair, the swagger in our steps, the particular way we can say "alright now" to fit our changing moods—Black culture saved me. It gave a little girl who was afraid of her own voice the language of identity. It cradled me when I needed a soft landing as a child. It challenged me as a teen. It emboldened me as a young adult. Blackness—our struggles alongside our deep joy, our pain, and our pride—is what wakes me up in the morning. It's my soul. So when I first met the "Queen of Soul" in 2003, to say I was in awe would be like saying the sun rises in the east.

That year BET was paying tribute to Ms. Franklin at our *Walk of Fame* benefit concert, which meant the company was putting on an entire weekend of celebrations in her honor. (The "Respect" singer required that everyone put plenty on her name. And *required* is the right word here. She didn't demand it or command it. It was simply expected.) Hollywood had its iconic Walk of Fame, and in keeping with one of Bob's favorite maxims—"Don't reinvent the wheel, just paint it Black"—in 1995 we decided to make our own. The annual tribute dedicated to musical giants was truly unlike anything Washington had ever seen before. The night was a grand production hosted and filmed in the cavernous soundstage at the company's new corporate headquarters in Northeast DC. It was a three-day-long celebration of exclusive VIP receptions, ladies' lunches, and red carpets all culminating in a star-studded black-tie concert. The whole affair was like a glitzy family reunion—if your family included Mariah Carey, Mary J. Blige, and Stevie Wonder.

The District didn't know what hit it. Before our show, the golden ticket was the annual Kennedy Center Honors hosted across town. That awards ceremony, venerable as it was, was not for or about us. At most, each year the Kennedy Center Honors would pay tribute to one Black honoree. The *Walk of Fame* was *our* night, in *our* city. This was some 13 years before the Obamas brought the A-list crowd to the boring and sleepy capital. Our concert was glitzy at a time when Washington didn't really do glitz. Comedian Jamie Foxx, who was then most famous for his hilarious sketches on *In Living Color*, hosted our first shows. The night was all Black, so very Black.

Our premise was straightforward—give them their flowers while they're still here. Because if we didn't honor our greats, groundbreaking artists who'd changed the face of the entertainment industry, then who would? As a bonus, the evening helped bridge the gaps among our core audience, which spanned generations. The old heads, as it were, were honored, and the newbies got to perform tributes to their heroes. John Legend made his very first television appearance at the *Walk of Fame* honoring Smokey Robinson. The young Mr. Legend sang Robinson's ethereal "Quiet Storm," and the crowd went nuts. "Who *is* that?" folks in the audience whispered as John crooned from his piano while a billowing mist rose from the stage. Smokey got up out of his seat. Before that night John was known solely as Kanye West's producer. *Walk of Fame* gave John one of his first chances to shine a little brighter. That was the extraordinary thing about BET: We could uplift our own. We could also be ourselves around each other.

Only BET could produce something like this—an event that was glamourous but somehow intimate. *Walk of Fame* was like a fancy family reunion complete with the added drama. Like the time I had to tell Bobby Brown he couldn't come to our Friday afternoon ladies' luncheon.

In 1996, we paid tribute to Whitney Houston, who was still riding the mega success of her film *Waiting to Exhale*. Whitney showed up to the sixth floor of BET's corporate headquarters where the luncheon was being held with her best friend and executive assistant Robyn Crawford, which was a relief. Leading up to the event the singer's team had been going back and forth with mine about a different plus one. Bobby Brown, Whitney's husband of four years and the self-proclaimed bad boy of R&B, wanted in. But there was just one problem: The afternoon was for women only.

"Well, that's not going to work," I told my assistant, Bobette. "Tell them no."

"But Bobby *really* wants to come."

"He can't." I wasn't budging. The big night belonged to the honoree and their friends and family. But the afternoon was for *us*, Black women. After a week of calls, Houston and Brown's camp finally conceded with a blunt "Okay, fine, Bobby won't come." I could practically hear the "My Prerogative" singer sulking somewhere in the background. Sorry, Bobby, no boys—bad boys included. In the end, Robyn escorted Whitney to the lunch, and we all had a fantastic time.

But that minor headache paled in comparison to dealing with *the* Aretha Franklin. A diva's diva if there ever was one. Over the years we'd toasted Smokey, Michael, Whitney, Diana Ross (whose hair is just as magnificent in person as it looks on-screen), Luther Vandross, Patti LaBelle, and Stevie Wonder, but Aretha? She left a permanent impression on me.

By the time our paths crossed, I'd been at BET for almost 17 years and had dealt with my fair share of divas onstage and difficult people in the wings. I'd been warned about Lady Soul. It was known that "No" was a complete sentence to Ms. Franklin (specifically when she was the one saying it). The icon knew what she wanted, how she wanted it, and exactly when you were to deliver it. Diva? Sure. But didn't she deserve it? Didn't any Black woman who'd survived the male-dominated music industry warrant a little runway when it came to so-called "demands"? Would a man in her shoes be labeled difficult? I remember mulling that over when I received my first message from the queen.

"Ms. Franklin would like a new winter wardrobe for the weekend," my assistant Bobette told me from her desk outside my office. I couldn't have heard that right.

"A what?" I asked.

"A full winter wardrobe," repeated Bobette, emphasizing each word.

"Doesn't she live in Detroit? Where she would have a winter wardrobe?" I asked. "Tell them we don't do that." Bobette was already picking up the phone as I walked back to my office chuckling to myself. A full winter wardrobe? Furs and hats and all? This woman was tripping. That was the first no, or, taken differently, that was the first time Ms. Franklin taught me something about advocating for yourself. There would be plenty more noes and lessons to come.

It was tradition for me to purchase a special gift for the Walk of Fame honoree every year. For weeks leading up to the event, my team and I would explore each celebrity's specific hobbies and tastes to find a meaningful token. Patti LaBelle was a shoe fanatic, and I found her some fabulous sparkling Jimmy Choo stilettos. Smokey Robinson loved golf, and Bob tracked down a pin flag from the Master's signed by the legendary Tiger Woods himself. I took my job as BET's diplomatic hostess very seriously, trying to ensure that each honoree received a gift that they truly would love. But then word came back that Ms. Franklin wanted a watch from the luxe diamond jeweler Harry Winston.

"I wish I could buy her a $50,000 watch," I told Bobette. "That's not gonna fly either." I figured a firm and solid "sorry but no" was needed. If I drew a line in the sand now, Ms. Franklin would get the message—I wasn't a pushover even when it came to the woman whose lyrics I had belted into my wooden hairbrush as a 12-year-old. Boy, was I wrong.

The Queen of Soul would personally phone my office to iron out the details of her weekend in Washington with me directly. This was run of the show stuff that, honestly, was a tad, shall we say, below my pay grade. Producers, stage managers, set designers, assistants. Those are the very capable and talented professionals being referred to when someone says, "I'll have my people call yours." No one expects the COO of the company to hash out seating arrangements over the phone. But Ms. Franklin did not bother with middlemen. She went straight to the top—me.

In the weeks leading up to the concert, whenever my phone rang, there was a 50–50 chance Ms. Franklin was on the other end. Our calls always began the same way: "Hello, Debra, it's Ms. Franklin," and then she'd launch into all the things I needed to do. Afterward I'd take a deep breath and get it done.

Did she like me, respect me, tolerate me? I could never figure that out.

And remember, there was still the matter of that $50,000 timepiece. Aretha's team came back with a compromise. Ms. Franklin, we were told, would accept a Chanel white enamel watch. Those were around $5,000, and I was happy to gift her one, and I hoped that once she got to DC it'd be smooth sailing. Why on earth did I think that?

The afternoon of the show we were informed that Ms. Franklin had lost all 60 of the tickets we'd given her for the concert and she required 60 replacement tickets. That was already an unusually high number for a charity event hosted in a venue that held 800. But Stephen had sold me on the "sure, no problem" solution. "Tell her we'll have more tickets waiting at the soundstage," I informed Bobette, who looked at me like I had three heads. "And make sure she knows that these new tickets will have the *exact* same barcodes as the ones she 'lost.' "

That night Ms. Franklin and I sat next to each other in the front row. She was a vision in a white organza ball gown and a poker face no queen could ever imitate. Yolanda Adams, Tamia, Seal, Norah Jones, the Isley Brothers, and more sang tributes to the Queen of Soul, and while she was always gracious, I could tell from my seat that she was itching to get onstage herself. My personal favorite was the Queen of Hip-Hop Soul, Mary J. Blige, whose rendition of "Natural Woman" came from someplace deep. When Mary belted out her last note, I leaned over to Ms. Franklin: "Wasn't that amazing?" The Queen responded without missing a beat: "Wait till I get up there." And, man, she wasn't lying. Ms. Franklin burned the house down. The crowd was on its feet in seconds. In the middle of her performance, during a spiritual rendition of "Today I Sing the Blues," she snatched her own wig and threw it to her security guard, who in turn put it on *his* head. In that moment, whatever headaches I had were swiftly forgotten, drowned out by the sound of that voice and the thundering applause.

But before all that Ms. Franklin told the audience that the past three days of celebrations in Washington had been the most "beautiful" of her entire career—bar none—and I believed her. She even thanked me personally from the stage, and my pride swelled. *Oh, Aretha*, I thought, shaking my head. There was no one else like her, and I felt privileged to have even a toe in her spotlight. But I still wasn't certain if we were, in fact, friends, and I realized in that moment that it actually mattered to me. There were very few examples of Black women surviving and thriving in the corporate and entertainment worlds. And by very few I mean zero. No wonder I didn't see myself giving orders instead of taking them. Not only was I a young woman, Black, and from the South, but I was also shy and needed to be liked. The climb to CEO was made even rougher by the lack of mentors who looked like me. Aretha was that for me whether she wanted to be or not, and I felt a kinship with her.

But that didn't mean the outlandish requests stopped.

As a general rule, BET didn't give airtime to talent acts we'd never heard of. But Ms. Franklin's grandson was a rapper, and she wanted him to perform during her mini concert for the BET Honors in 2014. In fact, she wouldn't get on her bus (the "Ain't No Way" crooner famously stopped flying in 1983 after a terrible experience on a two-engine plane) unless we agreed to let the young man share her stage. Oh, and she also had a granddaughter who could sing! Yep, she wanted her in the show too.

I called an emergency meeting in my office.

"Here's what we're going to do," said Stephen Hill, then the company's President of Music Programming and Specials. Stephen was a talented producer and could find a laugh within most challenges. He'd joined the company about a decade after I did and shared my vision for our future as a true driver of the culture. Stephen had boundless energy and always advocated for us to push the envelope. He had a crazy solution: "Tell her it's fine. We'll let them perform."

"Stephen, there's no way," I said. Had he lost his mind? "We don't even know if these kids can actually rap and sing. All those people in the audience. The donors? This could be a complete disaster."

Stephen gave me a reassuring look I'd grown familiar with over the years, "Debi, we can't run the risk of making an enemy out of Aretha Franklin. But don't worry about it. Those performances will never see the light of day." He taught me something that day about push and pull, the give and take of dealing with difficult people in power. You had to make them happy while also doing what was best for you. That is always the juggling act of a senior executive. That day we told Ms. Franklin "sure, no problem" and agreed to let her granddaughter and son have their moment in the spotlight—but the cameras would be off. Stephen's plan worked. Ms. Franklin eventually got on that bus.

A few years later, I ran into Ms. Franklin at Al Sharpton's birthday party in New York. Around that same time, a production team had been floating the idea of BET acquiring an old gospel concert she had recorded in Los Angeles in 1972. Everyone in the business knew Aretha was not a fan of the documentary, which had been gathering dust for decades. My general counsel, Darrell Walker, wanted to see if I could convince her to let BET air the recording. Did he know this woman? Aretha Franklin could not be convinced to do anything that Aretha Franklin did not want to do. But I tried anyway. When I spotted her at Al's, I pulled up a chair and asked her directly how she felt about the documentary. There was no use beating around the bush. Ms. Franklin wasn't a fan.

"I hate it," she told me. "I didn't like the creative team then, and nothing's changed. Debra, I never want it to be seen."

"Okay, Ms. Franklin," I said. Remembering our near-daily phones calls from years before, I easily slid into my role as her handler. "I'll take care of it." When I got back to Washington on Monday, I gave Darrell and the team my answer: "We can't." They, of course, pushed back. This was Aretha Franklin we're talking about! The film documented the live recording of one of her most successful albums to date. Acquiring it wouldn't just be a major get for the network but a major moment "for the culture." For the culture. I took a moment to reflect on what those three words really meant.

"Excuse me? Miss Lee?" The first time someone acknowledged my work for the culture I was fresh from the red carpet of a Hollywood gala honoring John Williams, the *Star Wars* composer, and looking for my seat inside the theater. As usual, I was one of the handful of Black people in the crowd, and a tuxedo-clad attendant spotted me from a mile away. He made a beeline in my direction from across the sparkling theater lobby, and I just knew there was something burning in his back pocket—a carefully folded résumé, a demo tape, a business prospectus, something. But what came out of his mouth left me speechless.

"Miss Lee," he ventured shyly, balancing a heavy plate of champagne glasses in one hand while clasping mine with the other hand. "I just want to say thank you for everything you're doing for the culture." I did a slight double take before thanking *him* for his support. I couldn't believe he was singling me out. Me? I always knew that the work I did had an impact that was deeply felt by our community even if I wasn't always the person on the front end of the camera. For me, working for BET wasn't just a job, it was part of my purpose. Still, in the beginning, I was always surprised when someone felt the same about my work.

The second time this happened, I was power walking the streets of New York, on my way to yet another *make it or break it* meeting at Viacom's offices in bustling midtown Manhattan.

The city's streets are no joke, and as I navigated my way through the ever-present crowds of sightseeing tourists and other business folks operating on turbo ambition toward Viacom's corporate HQ, a young Black man stopped me in my tracks and repeated that same line nearly word for word: "Thank you for doing it for the culture."

Another time I was at a Burberry fashion showcase at its flagship store off Fifth Avenue in Manhattan. One of the waiters recognized me. "I see you," he said. "I appreciate what you're doing for the culture," he added before disappearing back into the crowd filled mostly with men and women who looked nothing like us.

For the culture. It was a welcome reminder that my time at BET was decades well spent. That the blood, sweat, and tears I put in as general counsel, COO, and then CEO were not only worth it but wholly necessary. That climbing the corporate ladder to the pinnacle of a career in the entertainment industry was about lifting not just me, not just the 600 employees who worked tirelessly behind the scenes, but an entire people. And the fact that we did all of that for years on a shoestring budget while remaining authentically and unapologetically Black? Well, that was what these young fans were getting to the heart of. We—Bob Johnson, me, BET executives, talent, and employees—did it for the culture.

Those young men who approached me with their appreciation on display underscored one of the crucial ingredients to my success as a manager and CEO. Only an unshakable foundation can support a behemoth career, and I built mine on solid rock— my love for the culture. Before I joined BET as a young law firm associate, I always felt like I had to leave who I was outside the revolving glass doors of my office building. At the network, I got to bring my full self to work every day. I took my deeply personal understanding of Black people, Black power, Black music, Black art, and Black life and helped erect a business on top of it. Not despite it but because of it.

When you marry what you love with what you do, the work (because it *is* work) doesn't get easier, it gets lighter. Take a breath, dig deep, and decide what excites you. Then point your career toward it. Folks say that if you love what you do then you'll never work a day in your life. Well, that's not entirely true. Oh, you'll work all right. In fact, you'll probably work harder than you ever have before. But the blood, sweat, and tears will feel like a calling, not a chore. You'll be committed to something greater.

All that led me back to Ms. Franklin. I knew Darrell and his team were right. Buying the concert film would be a great business move. But would it be for the culture? Would it hurt the company more than it served the community? Would it hijack a legacy?

"It'd be incredible," I said. "And we're still not doing it."

This was Ms. Franklin's choice. If she didn't want the film shown, BET, which I believed should always be a safe space for Black voices, wouldn't be the network to buy it. I'd never exploit her like that, no matter how many dollar signs were involved. Folks in-house were disappointed, but I knew it was the right decision. It was a "no" and I owned it.

Amazing Grace wasn't released until after Ms. Franklin's death in 2018, and it quickly became a critical hit. I went to see it in the theater by myself. The young afro'd Aretha who stood on the pulpit dressed all in white, turning a small chapel into holy ground, was instantly recognizable as the grown woman I'd first met nearly 30 years later. Chills ran down my spine as I sat alone in my seat. Mixed in with my awe was more than a small amount of regret that BET wasn't the platform to bring it to the world, but

I never regretted backing Ms. Franklin's decision. I was acting as a CEO, a Black woman, and an ally.

That was the thing about BET—we were more than just a network. I was more than just another CEO. Our audience, the entertainment industry, and the culture as a whole expected more from us. And as a Black woman operating in a world that often did not value us, it was my responsibility to do as much as I could do to support other Black women. Not everyone lets a personal mandate like that order their climb up the ladder, but I did. Who I am and what I did were one in the same. And once I took a senior leadership role, I wanted everyone in the building to expect more from themselves. I'm sure we could've acquired the rights to *Amazing Grace* without Aretha's permission. But why would I do that to a Black artist? A Black woman? We had to do better. That was part of the brand, the business. Being better. BET had to be the standard bearer. It was the place where our people came to see their authentic selves, not where they came to be exploited.

After that I figured Ms. Franklin and I were at the very least on good terms—two powerful women who understood each other. Over the course of knowing her in both a professional and personal capacity, I could never get a read on whether we'd moved from mutual respect to *maybe* friends. But what I loved most about Ms. Franklin is that she always kept me on my toes. Case in point: She'd invited me to her 70th birthday party in New York. At the time I was dating an entertainment lawyer, who was also invited. Before the celebration, Ms. Franklin called my office to see if the two of us would be coming together. I said yes. But when we went to find our seats—at the Queen of Soul's head table, no less—we'd been split up. Her name was next to my date's, and my name was next to her fiancé's. Some of the other guests noticed and suggested we do some shuffling. Ms. Franklin didn't say anything about the swap when she joined the table, but a month later, she sent me a thank-you card with this note: "Thank you for coming to my birthday party, Debra. I see you moved your seat. I just wanted to let you know that it is customary for dates to be split up at a formal dinner party. I hope you're well. And thank you for the gift certificate to the Red Rooster but I am on a very strict diet." I laughed out loud when I read it. This woman was too much and more importantly always herself. But was that strike two for me? Did she like me? Were we friends?

In 2015, my assistant Bobette buzzed me to say that Ms. Franklin was on the line. I braced myself. "Debra," she said in that rich voice that made hearts melt and hairs stand at attention. "I'll be in DC for the attorney general's farewell ceremony at the Justice Department. Why don't you come as my plus one?" Ms. Franklin was Attorney General Eric Holder's favorite singer, and he'd personally asked her to perform at one of his first farewells. I needed zero convincing: "I'd be honored to come." What I didn't tell Aretha was that I'd already been invited to the ceremony. Eric and I were old friends. We'd met decades before as young Black lawyers who'd just arrived in DC to make our respective marks on the nation's capital. The AG had been a part of my inner circle for years. Heck, his wife, the incredible Dr. Sharon Malone, was my gynecologist. But if Aretha wanted me to roll with her? The answer was always yes.

"Debra, you've got to get out here," Bobette buzzed the night of the ceremony a few weeks later. Ms. Franklin would not be kept waiting. I immediately put down the contract I was mulling over, pushed my chair away from my massive glass desk, and walked over to my closet to grab a new pair of heels and statement necklace to take my gray sheath dress up a notch. I always kept chic after-five accessories in my office. As CEO, you never knew where you'd have to go and whom you'd have to meet outside the office. Plus Aretha loved jewelry, and I made sure to wear an eye-catching bauble when she was around. I left BET headquarters to meet the Queen of Soul in the lobby of the Mandarin Oriental. The two of us rode in a limo over to Main Justice together with a friend of hers from Detroit. Before she walked onstage, the three of us waited together in the green room while she got ready.

I was in awe, watching Aretha getting her hair primped, her lashes curled. I just remember it being easy between us. I didn't have anything to do besides enjoy being in her company. It was a rare glimpse into the kind of woman she was. There was no sign of a diva in that dressing room. Most celebrities are pretty finicky about whom they let into their inner circle, and there were few celebrities whose circles I wanted to be let into. But that hour before the concert was special. I knew then that Aretha thought of me as a friend and not just a fellow businesswoman or the lady who sat in the wrong seat at her birthday party. I saw the side of her that most don't. We chatted about Washington and politics, and Aretha loved my chunky silver necklace. She had impeccable taste in everything. She loved shiny, expensive things—diamonds, furs, watches, oh, and men. Ms. Franklin got a kick out of an attractive man. That evening in the green room she made no secret of the crush she had on Eric. "Isn't he handsome?" she said with a sly grin. This was the woman behind the microphone. It reminded me how we all have to put on a mask sometimes, taking on a persona to go out and do our jobs. Then I watched as she slowly began transforming from the Aretha who'd been laughing and joking with me in the limo into *the* Aretha Franklin. This was one of those good "pinch me" moments. That night she shared the stage with AG Holder and President Barack Obama, serenading the crowd with "America the Beautiful."

In the end—and, yes, I know it sounds cliché—she taught me

about respect. She always respected me enough to say exactly how she felt—good or bad. She didn't suffer fools or pull punches around anyone—high or low. In fact, I think she saw the two of us as equals. Of course, I didn't see it that way. This is Aretha. But I was another Black woman fighting to be seen and heard in an industry that often did neither. I was a businesswoman, and so was she. I spent my days navigating men who thought they knew more than I did. She'd spent decades doing the same. Aretha saw me in more ways than one and more ways than most others could. Her demands, her straight talk, her laughter all buoyed me. Our decades-long friendship—because in the end, I would call it that—was the epitome of doing it for the culture. The nexus of the work and the women behind it.

Demanding respect is a practice of self-love, not a problem. In the corporate world, women, Black women especially, have to fight for every inch of the space they take up. Ms. Franklin made no apologies about the room she required. And she recognized the fight in me. They say never meet your heroes lest they disappoint you, but Ms. Franklin proved the opposite of that maxim can be true too. Some heroes can let you down, but others can lift you up. Without knowing it, she'd given me a tremendous gift. She validated me. And I needed that from the moment we met. Our greatest teachers don't always know they're teaching. What Aretha never knew was that her unapologetic confidence wasn't just helping the grown-up Debra navigate a corporate world that didn't always see or hear her, it was also helping heal the little girl who was afraid of her own voice.

"Turn around and just sing, Debra!" yelled my ninth-grade chorus director. Once again, I had my back to the auditorium, enjoying the safer view of my best friend Saundra's face. Why this woman put me in the front row, I'll never know. Terrified of singing out loud and in front of actual people, I'd furiously turn my head away from the dreaded crowd. I was too nervous, too afraid. All those eyes staring at me? No, thank you. They could still hear me with my head turned, right?

I always knew I was shy, but it wasn't until I read Susan Cain's *Quiet: The Power of Introverts in a World That Can't Stop Talking* that I put a name to what I'd felt forever: "introverted."

Even today, I have fewer, closer relationships. I'm not my best in a large group. I get nervous before I meet anyone new, no matter how senior I am (or how junior they are). I'm fine when I'm on a panel, one of a bunch, but when the spotlight is shining on me and only me, that's when my palms start to sweat and my voice shakes. Public speaking, whether I'm presenting to a class or on a stage in front of thousands, remains hard. That old trick of feeling less vulnerable and nervous by picturing everyone in the crowd naked? Yeah, that never worked for me. What I learned over years and years of public speaking is that practice doesn't so much make perfect as it makes bearable. In fact, the idea of a multi-city tour to promote this very book you have in your hands, while thrilling, is also anxiety-inducing. I'll need plenty of help—the support of my incredible friends as conversation partners and the encouragement of the audience. Please someone nod your head. That's my trick— look for the one person in the crowd who's nodding along with you. That person, god bless him or her, gives me the confidence to keep going. But my stomach still churns. I still feel that wave of relief after I get to sit back down and I'm done having to talk. Once again, just a face in the crowd. That's when the knots loosen up a bit and I finally relax—that is, until the next time someone asks me to get up and open my mouth.

When I first met Aretha, I'd been COO of BET for nearly seven years, a much longer tenure than most number twos who would have moved on to a CEO position long before. But there was always something holding me back. I knew I was qualified and that my vision for the company moving forward was a solid one. But I also knew that the mountain I had to climb to get respect was steep and not everyone in the company was cheering me on along the way. Once the network's chief financial officer and I had to give a presentation about our fiscal standing for a group of analysts in New York. Our CFO, a white man who probably wanted my job, didn't like me. As soon as I dove into my presentation—a set of ordered slides and scripted cards I'd worked on for weeks—I knew something was wrong. All the slides had been rearranged, and I was left up there having to wing it—my worst nightmare. I was flustered and unnerved and sounded like it. And the whole time our CFO sat there looking especially satisfied as I struggled. I was convinced he mixed up my slides on purpose, and when I asked him about it, he smirked. I never mentioned it to Bob. I just made sure to always load my slides myself from then on.

I was "the nice one," and early on it felt like a handicap. I was the senior executive whose voice still quivered when she had to give a town hall speech in the same massive soundstage we used for the *Walk of Fame* concert. For a while I thought being quiet and shy meant I could never truly lead a big booming entertainment network like BET. And other folks thought it too. Just like the CFO, there were senior executives who knew my pain point was public speaking, and they made it their mission to do the absolute most anytime we had to host companywide meetings. There was this one executive who dressed up as a drum major and high-stepped down the aisle to the stage of a town hall meeting while throwing money into the crowd of employees shouting, "Cake! Cake! Cake! Cake! Cake!..." Yeah, that would never be me. Was it a weakness? Some of the men reporting to me seemed to think so, and they thought they had something on me. Heck, I thought it too for a while.

Women like Aretha helped. I borrowed her confidence whenever I had to step onstage. But more than that she also taught me that you didn't have to be anyone but yourself in order to command the room. In fact, you needed to be fully yourself to do it right, and that didn't mean dancing and carrying on. That's not who I am, and putting on a show wouldn't change that. On the flip side, being an extrovert—or a drum major—didn't automatically make someone a good leader. We worked behind the camera, remember? Eventually I did come to appreciate executives who wanted to shine as an extrovert or introvert and we were able to coexist on a leadership team. But for far too long the little girl in me, the one who was afraid to sing out loud, felt she was lacking in some way. That someone who preferred the background could never be CEO. Boy was I wrong.

"Debi, you're doing it all wrong. It's like this," said my friend Saundra as she corrected the steps I'd been quietly practicing in the corner. You couldn't tell Saundra, Sheila, and me that we weren't the Supremes-in-training. Whenever a new song climbed to number one on WEAL, the Black radio station in Greensboro, the three of us would rush to someone's bedroom after school and get to work choreographing a new routine. "Stop in the Name of Love," released in 1965, the year I moved to North Carolina, was one of our favorite combinations. I was always in the background though, too shy to step out front or sing loud enough for anyone not in my own head to hear.

As a kid I lived and breathed Black culture. Those knots I got in my stomach whenever I had to speak in front of my class? They went away when I was alone in my kitty-cat-themed bedroom singing the hits of the day for no one but the reflection in the mirror. "Stop in the Name of Love" was one of the first records I purchased from the record store on Elm Street, Greensboro Record Center. Rushing home to play it in my bedroom felt like freedom. That was my world, listening to the Supremes—and the Temptations, Smokey Robinson, the Four Tops, Stevie Wonder, Martha and the Vandellas, Aretha. Their voices were proud and bold. Their confidence stood starkly in opposition to my own. They epitomized what I dreamed of growing up to be, if only I could sing. Heck, if only I could speak.

If someone looked into a crystal ball and predicted that years later I'd be speaking on award show stages in front of thousands and broadcast for millions more, I wouldn't have laughed. I would have escaped to the nearest bathroom for an ugly cry. I persevered not by becoming someone else but by embracing who I was (plus practice, practice, practice). And borrowing more than a little of the confidence I admired in other women. Stepping into your flaws and all is the only way to lead. I learned that from the glamourous divas of my youth who became uncompromising legends decades later.

If you, too, were the kid who didn't want to sing in a chorus or are the adult who feels nervous about taking center stage to be successful, you aren't defective. There's nothing wrong with not wanting to be the center of attention. Shyness doesn't mean you aren't going to be successful; it means you just aren't cut out for the choir. CEO, though, that was something I was cut out for. Too often we ask children *what* they want to be when they grow up and not *who*. Well, somehow, I'd managed to do both. What I did was who I was.

"Hey, aren't you that BET lady?" That question always made me chuckle. I spent three decades at the company. I'd handed out awards and won more than a few myself. I'd helped shape careers on and off the screen. I'd advised presidents and been protested

against. And folks still didn't know my name. Debra Lee? Please. I would forever and always be "that BET lady."

It never failed. Strangers would notice my now-signature short blond curls and squint their eyes in recognition. "Heeey, aren't you...?" But no one could ever get past the BET part of who I was. If folks wanted to call me "that BET lady," then let them. I'd earned it.

What's funny is that I never *ever* saw myself as the person in charge. Growing up (and, let's be honest, well into adulthood) I saw myself as a backup singer, not the lead. The background was quiet, comfortable. The 11-year-old who sped through her chores early every Saturday morning in order to sit in front of the living room TV and watch the impossibly smooth Don Cornelius interview Smokey Robinson never could have imagined that one day she too would stand in rooms with those big names and call some of them friends.

The culture. It's what broke me out of my shell time and time again. It's what led me to commit my life to telling Black stories, creating original programming, and offering that feeling that I used to get seeing a reflection of myself on-screen and in pictures. Doing it for the culture is what gave me the strength and confidence to leap past my "nice girl" hang-ups and learn how to put my foot down with the best of them—ahem, Ms. Aretha Franklin. Knowing your worth, how to command (not demand) respect, and how to say no with love were business lessons the Queen of Soul taught me just by being herself. She showed me what power looked like. That it could be wrapped up in a mink coat and topped with a curly wig while wielding just as much influence and impact as the guys in the suits. Aretha showed me that the things *we* loved, our culture—music, dance, and art and Black life presented in bright colors and loud, clear voices—was power.

CHAPTER TWO

FEMALE CEO STATUS

"They're protesting me?" I complained to my girlfriend Yolanda as she placed one of her famous sweet potato pancakes on my plate, comforting me in her kitchen because my own home no longer felt like mine. Nearly 200 protestors were gathered outside my house shouting about how terrible BET was into bullhorns. The demonstrators had arrived late that morning. Hundreds of people—the entire congregation of a Maryland church—spilling out of buses brandishing signs that read "I'M NOT A WHORE" or "I'M NOT A BITCH" as they marched up and down the sidewalk at my address near Embassy Row. My neighbors were indignant. I, on the other hand, was devastated.

"Me? But I'm Debra Lee. I actually care!" Yolanda nodded her head and added another pancake to the pile.

"Don't worry, Debi," she said. "You know how these things go. Folks get mad. They make a fuss. Then next week someone else becomes the target and everybody moves on. Things will be back to normal before you know it."

I wanted to believe her. I really did. But they kept coming. Every single solitary Saturday. For. Seven. Months. Whenever I'd hear the familiar crackle of a megaphone, I'd think to myself, *This is what happens when a woman is in charge.*

It was 2007, and I had finally taken the reins as CEO of BET, a hard-won promotion nearly 20 years in the making. Bob had resigned the year before, and after being his number two for the better part of my career, I was more than ready to step out of his very long shadow and into the spotlight—or at least my version of it. Being the center of attention still gave me goosebumps. Companywide town halls made my palms sweat, and my voice quivered during speeches. Senior staff meetings were rocky as the male executives, who'd been loyal to Bob and how we *always* did things, chafed against my new vision for the company.

It's fair to say that in the beginning it was shaky at the top and the ground beneath my title was anything but solid. That's a fact of leadership that rarely gets talked about. The promotion is just the starting line. Your title doesn't immediately confer respect, and it doesn't come with clear instructions, especially for female senior executives who unfortunately have fewer footsteps to follow. Learning the hard way for us sometimes is the only way. But I never imagined my first public pop quiz as CEO would come so soon after moving into the corner office. And I definitely didn't think folks would be rallying outside my front door, demanding the very change I'd been trying to implement behind the scenes for what felt like my entire tenure at BET. But I couldn't tell the demonstrators that—yet. The pressure had been building for years, and all it took was one meeting to burst the pipe.

His name was Delman Coates, and he was the young new pastor of Mt. Ennon Baptist, a growing church about a 30-minute drive outside the District in the suburbs of Maryland.

"There's a Reverend Coates who wants to talk to you," Bobette informed me one busy morning in between meetings. As CEO I had major plans to usher in a new era of original and inspirational programming. I wanted us to stop relying so heavily on music videos and the mercurial artists behind them and to start creating our own content. We had the talent and the drive to truly become a network with a voice like the legacy cablers attracting movie stars to the small screen and snatching up statues during awards season. After decades of laying the groundwork, it was time to start building a more elaborate vision for the company's future. "Just paint the wheel Black," Bob's old business model, wasn't going to cut it forever.

Barack Obama, a dynamic Democratic senator from Illinois, was getting closer to the White House than any Black candidate who had come before him. Major cable networks had finally figured out that Black audiences weren't niche because the ratings, subscriber numbers, and subsequent ad dollars didn't lie. There were industry rumblings that Oprah and Magic Johnson were gearing up to start their own networks. The ground was shifting. Like any business, if BET wanted to thrive, the network would have to evolve beyond using Blackness as a brand strategy. We had to have true principle. We had to create a belief system. Crafting that vision would be one of the most difficult tasks of my career and my greatest achievement at BET—a Herculean task that combined every lesson (good and bad) I'd ever learned from my military father on up to the head honchos at Viacom. But first I'd have to deal with yet another man.

"Debra?" Bobette said.

"Hmm..." I'd been lost in thought, trying to pull together all the threads I knew I needed to make this brand relaunch work. "I'm sorry. Who?"

"Coates. He has a church out in Maryland, and apparently he isn't happy with some of the music videos we've been showing lately. 'Duffle Bag Boy' came up." Once again one of the videos we aired was getting the company into hot water. This time it was hip-hop duo Playaz Circle's single featuring rapper Lil Wayne causing trouble with a song that made none-too-veiled references to drug dealing and drug use. It wasn't one of my favorites, to say the least. But I also strongly believed in their individual right as artists to rap about whatever they wanted to and our company's right to broadcast the video as long as it wasn't violating any of the FCC's regulations. Through the years BET had aired plenty of music videos that made grandmothers clutch their pearls, but our motto was simple: as long as it doesn't break any rules. My personal taste wasn't in the equation—yet. Also, I couldn't help but wonder why this pastor was calling to complain now and not a year ago when Bob was in charge. Did he assume that a female CEO would bend more easily?

"Set up the meeting," I told Bobette before heading into one of my own.

Reverend Coates was waiting for me when I walked into the glass conference room down the hall from my office. Normally I'd have Stephen or one of the EVPs tag along for meetings like this to make sure the company followed up afterward with whatever ask we could and to make sure I didn't overpromise anything. This time I had my EVP and General Counsel, Byron Marchant, sit in. I also figured this man runs a church. *How bad could it get?* The big guy in the black suit standing guard at the door (of *my* office building) should've tipped me off. He brought his own security? Oh, this pastor isn't playing.

"Ms. Lee, you know why I'm here," said Coates, wasting zero time. Ever the preacher, he launched into a sermon about the negative images that BET was promoting by playing certain videos. As a Black company, we should do better, he told us, completely unaware that while I agreed with him on the network's larger responsibility to the community, there was no way I would let this one man dictate to me about how to run my company.

First of all, I told him, we have a standards and practices committee. We reviewed every video on our air. We didn't allow profanity, we blurred out guns, and we tried to work directly with record labels when it came to how women were being portrayed on-screen. But that wasn't enough for Coates. Any videos that had anything to do with drug use had to go. Three videos in particular were in his sights, but "Duffle Bag Boy" was the one that stood out.

"That's clearly about drugs," he said from across the table. "We want that off the air."

"Listen, we're not going to analyze the lyrics of every song we play. And do you remember 'Cloud Nine' by the Temptations? 'Strawberry Fields Forever' by the Beatles? Clearly about drugs," I countered. Was this guy serious? Were song lyrics really the issue here?

"We're fed up, Debra. I want these three videos off the air," he repeated. "And if they don't come down, we're going to make our voices heard—loudly."

Power, in my view, doesn't come from shouting, sarcasm, or threats. A leader is the woman who doesn't need to do any of those things to get her point across and her directives followed. Nice I may be, but pushover I am not.

"If I let you take three videos off the air this month, you'll be back with three more videos next month," I told him. He seemed slightly taken aback. My tone hadn't changed, but my demeanor certainly had. Again, I didn't have to shout. If anything, my voice lowered so that he'd really have to sit up and pay close attention to hear the very important words coming out of my mouth. My gaze sharpened. My shoulders squared off. If he thought he could dictate terms, he had another thing coming. I'd carved out an hour of my day to sit down with this man and truly listen despite his threats, but the respect clearly wasn't reciprocal. He said jump and I was supposed to ask how high. That wasn't going to work for me. Not this time—or ever. There were no inches to give. The second I ceded any control over the programming at my company, I would be a target. I locked eyes with Pastor Coates from across the table and gave him my final answer: "I run this network, and you don't."

The thing with leaders like Pastor Coates is that they assume their title will do the talking for them. They assume that everyone will simply fall in line without earning the right to be followed. They assume that women will bend because they aren't trained to fight for what they believe in. They assume. It's a weakness that leaves them wide open for a surprise.

I don't think he ever believed I would do anything but back down. He assumed I'd rather give up some of my power in order to avoid a publicity headache. He was wrong.

A few weeks later, on a Saturday in mid-September, Pastor Coates kept his word. Early that morning some 250 protestors piled into buses around the area headed for my house in the District. They called themselves the Enough Is Enough campaign.

They'd had enough of BET, music videos, the media, and me. I'd been given a heads-up the day before. Thankfully my daughter, Ava, was spending the weekend with her dad, and my son, Quinn, was away at college. That left me alone waiting for a massive crowd of angry people to show up at my door. Sure, I was anxious. But I was also ticked off.

Bob had been running the company for decades, and no one had said boo to him about "saving the soul of America."

You know what I did on day one as CEO? I pulled the plug on *BET Uncut*, the raw and raunchy late-night music video show that no one would miss (well, except Patti LaBelle, who told me she loved it and had a bone to pick with me for canceling it—go figure). But no one *else* had anything to say about that. At least not to me.

I *was* doing the work behind the scenes to elevate the brand, but until all my ducks were in a row, I couldn't announce the new BET to the world just yet. I was fully aware of the enormous influence and responsibility we had as the leading purveyor of Black images. It's the reason I'd stayed at the company for so long—I'd committed to work because I saw it as something greater. Our network couldn't only be concerned with dollar signs. We should be a mirror, a safe space, and a launching pad. But I couldn't explain all of that to the folks gathering outside my home. It would be a major rebranding, and one of the first rules of corporate engagement is to keep your cards close to the vest until it's time to show and prove. And another thing, why were they at *my* door? Why not picket outside Nelly's house? Or Lil Wayne's? In fact, I had no problem with the campaign rallying outside BET's headquarters Monday through Friday. But I lived in Washington, which, as the seat of government, had some of the country's most lenient protest permitting laws.

"We are here today outside of the home of Debra Lee, but I want to be clear this campaign is not a campaign about a personality. This campaign is not a campaign about a company," said Reverend Coates into the mic set up on the corner of my block as the crowd sporting T-shirts emblazoned with red stop signs that read "Enough Is Enough" clapped and cheered. Over the weeks, comedian Dick Gregory would show up, along with civil rights activist C. Delores Tucker, who famously crusaded against gangsta rap, going head-to-head with Tupac and Suge Knight. They said they weren't protesting Debra Lee, but they could've fooled Debra Lee. They were waving signs and shouting slogans at my house. There were megaphones, the news media, it was a mess. Fortunately, I wasn't there.

My good girlfriend Yolanda Caraway, a highly respected political strategist and publicity maven, had heard about the impending doom and phoned me the day before with an invitation to her house. "I'll make sweet potato pancakes," she said, knowing that I needed to be anywhere but alone in my living room that Saturday morning. Before my block was swarmed, I grabbed my purse and headed to Yolanda's for some much-needed care and ranting. Sitting at her kitchen counter, I tried to reconcile my responsibilities with my purpose. I was the CEO of a major media company and was beholden to both our audience and our parent company, Viacom. I was also a Black woman who believed wholeheartedly that the images we put out in the world were just as important as, if not more so than, our bottom line. BET was more than a company. We had our community and our corporate interests to consider. The tightrope was steep but not impossible to tiptoe across.

"Trust me, people have short memories. This will blow over eventually, Debi," said Yolanda, a communications whiz who'd already started making calls to some of our influential friends behind the scenes, encouraging them to come out in support of me and the network. Because of her, Cornell West, Congresswoman Maxine Waters, and several hip-hop ministers (who knew they existed?) crossed the proverbial picket line. But it was still my name being dragged through the mud.

Folks were fired up, and the blaze was aimed at me. As the head of the company, I would always be in the hot seat. That was the job. Still, I hated the *us* versus *them* dichotomy. Picking a side seems so easy. Arguments are black and white. Gray areas are for giving in. But I felt like we, as Black people, were all on the same side. I wanted what they wanted—for BET to send not just positive but authentic messages out into the world. But as a leader I couldn't just shout and stomp my feet and get things done. There was so much heavy lifting behind the scenes that had to happen before the big kumbaya moment. That's what being the woman in charge meant—doing the work and not just the celebrating. Making the decisions that on their face looked suspicious, like two steps backward, but in the end get you to the finish line. It's hard as the woman in charge to swallow the bitter pill of doing the unpopular thing that gets you booed instead of applauded. But a leader isn't at the top to be praised; she's there to get the job done. It's a shift in thinking that requires lots of humility. Trust me, I know.

Coming of age in the segregated South idolizing Angela Davis and Malcolm X, I used to be staunchly opposed to surrender. No justice, no peace! That fight helped sharpen who I was. The idealism was necessary to make me into a woman with the kind of moral code and belief system that could withstand a protest outside her door decades later because she knew in her heart of hearts she was doing the right thing. That didn't mean it didn't sting, though, just that I was tough enough to keep going. I imagine it's how my dad felt about my teenaged activism and my opposition to so many of the decisions he was making at the time about my education and my future. Because just like the protestors gathering outside my door every Saturday morning, 16-year-old me thought I knew better than everybody, especially my dad, who clearly didn't realize the revolution was coming. Sometimes it felt like the two of us weren't breathing the same air. See, back then the NAACP convinced my dad and a few of the other Black parents at my high school to sue the Greensboro school system to end school segregation. Trouble was my friends and I had our own potential protest going, and it was called Save the Black School. My dad and I were polar political opposites at the time. My friends and I wanted a revolution, and our parents wanted to integrate. He thought I was naive, and I thought he was kowtowing to the system. Sound familiar?

My earliest memories are of my father pushing me to be better and to achieve more, especially when it came to school. Major Richard M. Lee was a man who didn't just dream big, he believed in laying the groundwork to get you there. He was a career military man, but he'd always wanted to be a lawyer despite never getting the chance to finish college. So, of course, Dad decided when I was in sixth grade that I was headed to law school. As the youngest child, I was his last hope. He told me I had to work hard, twice as hard as my white peers, and that I had to be better than everyone else. "Good" meant being the best. My father was not a loving man in the traditional sense, but he loved me and my potential. And he held me to it. He instilled an unrelenting drive for excellence, coupled with a fear of being anything less. Anything less than "good" meant that you weren't good enough. Excellence was the baseline because if you were Black, you didn't have another option.

He even made me a deal.

"Debi, I'll give you one dollar for every A you earn," he announced one day. I was in the sixth grade and already scoring high marks, but the idea of my own money (more Motown records!) motivated me. And when my teachers started breaking down large subjects into subcategories like writing and spelling for English, I made sure to get a dollar for each of those A's too. Dad grumbled about it, but I got that extra dollar. School meant everything to him. In fact, it's what brought us to the South in the first place.

In 1965 my father decided to retire from the army and finally get the college degree he'd dreamed of since he was kid. His brother-in-law coached football at North Carolina Agricultural and Technical State University, and my uncle pulled some strings to get Dad a job as a "house father" on campus. The position would allow our family of four (my big sister was away at college, which left me, my big brother, and our parents) to save money living in the dorms while Dad finished his bachelor's degree for free. The arrangement ended up being too good to be true. When we arrived in Greensboro that August, my father took one look at our decrepit dorm-style apartment and said, "I can't have my family here." Instead, we moved to Cumberland Court, one of the first nonprofit apartment complexes for low-income families built in the United States. That was Dad. He refused to let us settle for anything less than what we deserved. But he constantly reminded us that we weren't "better" than anyone.

"The people ain't no better than the folks. Remember that," he'd always say.

I kept Dad's advice in mind during the "Enough Is Enough" campaign against me. As Black folks we were all in the same boat. We all wanted the same things: to be validated, to be valued. We just saw two different paths to that goal. But the people, as Dad said, were no better than the folks. I didn't want to pit us against each other. Heck, I understood where they were coming from. But I tried to remember what Dad said when I was dealing with the protestors. They were our target audience. I couldn't talk down to them; I had to reach them somehow. We started in an unlikely venue: the United States Congress.

About a month into the protest, Congressman Bobby Rush held a congressional hearing on the effects of rap lyrics called "From Imus to Industry: The Business of Stereotypes and Degradation," referring to shock jock Don Imus, who was fired by CBS Radio after insulting Black women on air. My boss, Viacom's president and CEO Philippe Dauman, testified alongside other music and entertainment executives, plus rappers Master P and David Banner.

"We have a responsibility to speak authentically to our viewers," said Philippe, adding that we took our responsibility to our audience seriously, editing out excessive violence and vulgarity when necessary. But, Philippe added, "we also believe that it is not our role to censor the creative expression of artists."

That's right! I thought from my seat a few rows behind Philippe, satisfied that we were getting our say in the court of public opinion. I took a scan of the room to see other heads nodding in approval and more than a few shaking in disbelief. And there, of course, was Reverend Coates, looking more than a little satisfied himself. I had a feeling that he was behind the sudden political interest in what BET was doing. "We have to get out in front of this," I said to my team when the protestors started showing up.

The night of the congressional hearing, which in the end didn't do more than kick up dust, BET aired a three-part series titled "Hip-Hop vs. America." Rappers, activists, journalists, and preachers showed up to debate the state of the genre and its impact. Most everyone we called to participate said yes imme-diately. That is, except for St. Louis rapper Nelly, whose risqué music video "Tip Drill" had caused one of the network's biggest public relations headaches. I'd never seen it or that infamous scene where Nelly swipes a credit card through a woman's backside, but I knew he needed to be there. He didn't want the heat though. The video's director, Benny Boom, was coming, but the rapper kept making excuses. That's when I called him personally.

"If you don't come, you won't be supporting me, and that would make me very...unhappy," I told the "Country Gram-mar" singer over the phone. I was not the kind of leader who felt the need to throw her weight around. A flex is unnecessary if you have real muscle. I was one of the most powerful women in enter-tainment media—controlling one of the vital links between the rapper and his fans. He knew the risks.

"Alright, Ms. Lee," he said.

The ratings for the two panels that aired on BET were middling at best, but it wasn't about that. We'd gotten our point across. "The people were no better than the folks." We were listening. The open communication between my audience and my network was important to me. I knew what it was like to be a young per-son charged up on revolution and wanting change right now.

—

"You look just like Angela Davis," said Dad as I bounced into the kitchen for breakfast one morning before school. According to him I looked like "one of those radicals." What a compliment! I had hair the size of a beach ball, and I loved it. That morning I woke up an hour earlier than usual to carefully take down dozens of pink sponge rollers and fluff my thick hair until my coils were shaped into a perfect full moon. It was glorious—and my father was furious.

"It's dangerous, Debi. The FBI is looking for her. The FBI. She's on the run. A wanted woman. What's going to happen when they mistake you for her on the street? They could just snatch you up anytime," he said, snapping his fingers for emphasis. Okay, fine, he might've been right. Davis and I did sort of favor each other then. We were both fair-skinned with giant hair. That was more than enough for a white police officer who was likely to shoot first and ask questions later. I didn't care though. Nothing my dad could say would have stopped me from walking out of the house looking like my favorite radical. From the trauma of leaving our former home of Compton, California, right after the Watts riots to the comfort of our Black enclave in Greensboro, fighting for and deeply loving my community were becoming part of who I was. And I wanted folks to know just how down I was. It started with that afro.

In 1971, the Greensboro school board floated the idea of integrating my all-Black high school. They wanted to bus in white kids and hire white teachers. My classmates and I were up in arms. Of course, we knew that Dudley High didn't have a fraction of the resources the white high schools in town did, but for us, the solution was obvious. We needed more money, not white folks. Our parents though, they were all for it. Seeing the forest instead of the trees, they knew that a more integrated school system would mean bigger budgets for everyone. But we didn't see it that way. It was us versus them. Black versus white. So we came up with a plan: "Save the Black School!"

What I didn't know is that my father, who'd always been involved with the NAACP and worked for years in fair housing, had already signed on as one of the complainants in a lawsuit filed against the school district that would force integration and support the busing policy. I was so embarrassed when I found out, but it didn't stop my conviction that our school was a safe space that needed protecting. Of course, we didn't call them safe spaces then, but that's what it was. Looking back, it's no wonder that years later I would be so committed to turning BET into a safe space of its own. Because I knew the power of a place of your own. Dudley High was that. A brick building where, as Black children, we were challenged *and* cared for. It was a feeling we couldn't put into words for our parents, themselves children of the Jim Crow South who'd been forced to make do with less than nothing and wanted us to have an easier path to success. They were trying to initiate change from the inside out. The Debra who'd just taken over BET could relate. Oh, and did I mention a small group of protestors showed up at Philippe's townhouse off Park Avenue in New York City? Luckily, my boss was always supportive but I know he wanted his Saturdays back too.

For months the protestors wouldn't let up. Every Saturday Reverend Coates bused his congregation to my sidewalk to shout about how hip-hop was ruining our youth. I never once wanted to stop them from demonstrating—okay, fine, I wished it would all go away, but I recognized their right to speak their truth to power. But couldn't they do it Monday through Friday? I had no problem with them carrying on in front of BET Headquarters in Northeast DC. But my house? That made the whole thing feel like a personal attack despite Reverend Coates's claims that his problem wasn't with me but with the network. I could almost believe him, until they came for my daughter.

For months my family and I had been planning our Saturdays around the protests, which had become like a heavy blanket draped over our home life. I was a single mother by then, and as all single parents know, the schedule is sacrosanct. One morning we got our wires crossed and my daughter Ava, her babysitter, and our dog, Penny, left the house just five minutes before the crowd normally cleared out for the day. And do you know these adults followed my child, my 12-year-old, down the block, chanting, "I'm not a bitch"? When I returned home later that afternoon, Ava told me about it and how scared she was. I hugged my child tight and then immediately got on the phone with BET's general counsel.

"Okay, enough is really enough," I told Byron. "This is getting completely out of hand. Protest me all you want. But yelling at my baby? Absolutely not. What are we going to do about it?"

Byron started meeting with the city's officials behind the scenes to convince them to reevaluate the District's liberal protest laws and tighten noise ordinances in residential neighborhoods at least. But the city, filled with embassies, wouldn't budge.

"This is dangerous. Debra is a single mother. What if one of these people decides to come back late at night? What happens then? Whose fault would that be?" Byron pleaded our case. But Washington was Washington. The Massachusetts Heights neighborhood where I lived was filled with gorgeous late 19th-century buildings and nearly 100 diplomatic missions, which meant that there was no way around the protestors. Even if the city wanted to try to change the rules, enforcing something like that would be nearly impossible with an embassy on nearly every block. Byron kept coming back with the same answer. "They're not going to do anything."

"Not even about the bullhorns? The megaphones?"

"No."

We'd exhausted all of our options. After a few months, the crowd had dwindled from hundreds to maybe a few dozen. But the demonstration was still a source of pain for me. Especially as I was trying so hard to change things from the inside of BET HQ.

The network had been showing these very same videos for

decades, but suddenly it was all my fault. And on top of that, none of the artists the campaign was protesting came to my defense publicly or privately. Lil Wayne, Nelly, Ludacris, Jay-Z? I don't remember missing any of their calls. Internally we had even floated the idea of a counterprotest, steeped in the First Amendment and the artists' right to autonomy, but no one would get on board with it. They were more than happy to sit back and let me bear the brunt of all the bad press. It was at that point in my tenure as CEO that I realized playing small or nice wasn't going to cut it. Win or lose, as the head of the company it was all on me.

The one thing I remained firm on was never caving to Coates's demands. That wasn't going to happen. Every so often a representative from the church called to remind me, "We can make this stop anytime, Ms. Lee." And my response was always the same: "I'm not taking those videos off the air." That bravado? That audacity? It was hard-won. And it started in Greensboro at Dudley High with me holding my own protest sign high above my own head. Saying no again and again to Reverend Coates was my own personal protest. I wasn't going to give in because I knew I was right. I also knew that the fight was just as important as the outcome. Not only did he need to hear me say no, he needed to know that I wasn't backing down, I wouldn't be bullied. The power of standing in the truth of my own convictions was a lesson I first learned in high school.

The air feels charged when a group of like-minded people gather together for a cause. The atmosphere crackles; tiny sparks connect you to one another like the embers of iron sharpening iron. I'll never forget the first time I felt that energy. As a headstrong teenager, the air was thick with possibilities. That feeling of doing something? Saying something? Turning silence into action? I'd tap into it whenever I needed to be reminded and recharged.

It was a school night when our parents gathered in Dudley's auditorium to discuss the impending lawsuit and what it would mean. All that week a group of us had been meeting in the hallways and the bathrooms at school, plotting how we'd make our voices heard.

"Are we really going to do it?" Saundra (it was always Saundra) whispered to me during history class.

"We have to, right?" answered my other girlfriend Sheila from her desk behind mine.

"What other choice do we have? This is our school," I said, "and we can't let them just decide for us." I was starting to get used to this newfound bravado I'd discovered within myself.

The three of us geeked each other up. Straight-A students, we were terrified that a protest and the consequences that followed would look bad on our college applications, but we'd been backed into a corner. I knew my father would be on the warpath afterward, but the fire in my belly wouldn't cool down. We were young and idealistic and more than a little immature, but movements had moved mountains with less.

A few days later, as our parents settled into Dudley's auditorium to debate the merits of the lawsuit, we gathered outside with the signs we'd spent secret hours making at school. A parent had just stood up to address the crowd when Sheila, who'd been inside waiting for the meeting to start, gave us the signal. "Now," she mouthed, poking her head through the double doors. That's when a group of about two dozen of us marched into the room and down the aisles shouting, "Two four six eight! We don't want to integrate!" and "Save the Black School!" The look on the grownups' faces! I know they sat there thinking, *What on earth are these kids talking about?* The whole thing was over in less than five minutes. We trooped up and down the aisles with our fists in the air and our signs over our heads, certain that we were finally getting our point across. I stole one glance in my dad's direction to gauge how deep the water I'd gotten myself into was. He just stared, eyes narrow and mouth in a thin line. *Oh, boy,* I thought. *This wasn't going to be good.*

Our group stomped out of the room, and our parents went on with their meeting. An hour later in the parking lot, my father didn't say one word to me about what had happened inside. On the car ride back to Carlton Avenue, I tried to start a conversation— "But Dad—"—and he shot me that look. The one every Black child in America is all too familiar with. It said everything without saying anything. The matter was closed. We drove home in silence.

By my senior year, white kids were walking the halls of Dudley High. It just didn't feel right. Back then Black people and white people in Greensboro didn't mix—at all. They lived on their side of town, and we lived on ours. We didn't go to the same record stores, ice cream shops, or basement parties. To suddenly see these kids at *our* school? Something special had been taken from us, and no one, particularly our parents, seemed to care. But it was the law, and we adjusted—or at least tried to. And did I mention that I got my first D ever that semester? From a white teacher? I wanted to go home and show my dad, who'd never stopped giving me a dollar for every A, and say, "See? See? I told you integration wasn't gonna help." But I knew better than that.

We'd lost the battle, but the thrill of being a part of something larger than myself would never go away. "Save the Black School" had just been the beginning. I joined every active protest and demonstration I could find. They were mostly small acts of resistance, some of which were effective while others were, well, misguided. But I was growing into myself—figuring out what was important to me, my community, and my future. It was the beginning of a belief system that would carry me through every major decision I made going forward, from the personal to the professional. It's easy to say follow your passion, do what you love, and work woke. But first you have to figure out what you truly believe in and how that purpose fits into the larger story of who you are. My purpose was my people. Which is why when the revolution marched up to *my* door, it felt like falling out of the sky.

One day it all just stopped. I used to refer to the hours between 1 and 3 p.m. on Saturdays as my good nap time. I was joking, of course. Who could sleep when hundreds of people were shouting on your sidewalk? The point was I'd tried to tune them out and hold onto my peace. But on this particular Saturday in April, no one showed up. Silence.

What bothered me the most about the entire ordeal was that I always felt like I'd been doing the right thing. I was trying to get more money for original programming. I was trying to reduce the number of hours of music videos. I was trying to change, and things were just getting started when this guy came along.

One of the biggest lessons I learned from this period of my life—a lesson people rarely want to hear—is that change takes time, and you have to be committed to the ride, not just the finish line. And because of that, you have to be ready for the criticism. Reimaging BET's core values was like changing the tires of a plane in midair. We were a network with 24 hours of programming that consisted primarily of music videos. We didn't have a big budget or even the people skills to do original programming.

It was completely unchartered territory for us. So I knew the mission would take years. The big win was on the horizon, not in arm's reach. It would take *time*—the one resource people have so much of and don't know it.

To deal with the stress and pressure of not being able to get everything done all at once, I concentrated on small wins. I made incremental changes as quicky as possible to have a jolt of success and triumph. That's why I canceled *Uncut*. Success comes in small bites. Every year I improved our programming. We went from music videos to reality TV to scripted dramas. I couldn't just snap my fingers and make everyone happy.

In the end, the protest against me and the network was motivating. While it made my mission of turning around BET that much harder—I was already a woman and Black, trying to plot an uncharted course—it also helped sharpen my focus. Every day felt like a fight, and it made me more intent to remake the company. Not to impress these people, but to prove that the path I'd been on was the right one. Outside noise can be impossible to tune out, even when you're buried deep in the process of getting things done. But whether you're rebuilding a brand or creating something entirely new, you can't stop what you're doing to appease the critics because there will always be critics—there should be, in fact. Good leaders take their consumers' feedback to heart, but you can't let it consume you. Otherwise, the customers are running the company, not you. Instead, stay the course. Be patient with yourself. Get used to the intense heat whether you're at the top, on your way there, or just starting out because it's coming. Whenever you try to do anything differently, dissenting opinion will pop up in your path. Just don't let it slow you down.

CHAPTER THREE

THE CLIMB

So much of my success has been built on making the right decisions despite the fact that they looked wrong to most. Envisioning not just the finish line but how to get there—whether it took five years or fifteen—is a singular talent of mine. One that took years to hone, sharpening decision after difficult decision. Knowing my story and sticking to it has been a guiding light in my life. But standing up for my choices didn't come easy.

"Debra," said my father from his seat directly across from mine at the dinner table overflowing with baked ham, roasted turkey, simmered greens, and every other fixing a proper Southern Christmas feast would have. "Can I see you in the other room for a moment?" *Uh-oh,* I thought. Dad wasn't happy.

Ernie, my boyfriend, squeezed my hand beneath the lace tablecloth his mother had pressed to perfection that very morning. The two of us had been dating for about five months, and we'd just made a big announcement to the group of family members gathered at his parents' stately home in Jackson, Tennessee.

We'd met the year before while I was a senior at Brown and he was a senior at Harvard. I had a major crush on a fellow classmate named Isaac, one of Ernie's good friends. After a very, very brief fling with Isaac ended terribly, Ernie, who'd always been kind to me, was there to pick up the pieces. When I arrived on Harvard's campus the following September as a first-year law student, it was Ernie who volunteered to show me around Cambridge and Boston. I was in a funk those first weeks, struggling with the transition from Brown's egalitarian educational approach to the cutthroat competition of Harvard Law.

One morning in September, Ernie and I sat at a café in Harvard Square—he'd been taking me around to his favorite haunts for weeks—and started talking about what we were looking for in a romantic partner. I was over Harvard guys already. "I just want someone supportive, you know? Someone who gets how hard all of this is and instead of trying to prove how smart he is all the time is actually just there for me," I confessed in between sips of coffee.

"A girl who's nice," said Ernie about what he was looking for. "Someone with a good head on her shoulders." It didn't take long for us to figure out we were talking about each other. And that was that. We were an item from that moment on.

A few months in, we decided we didn't like living in the graduate dorms. The culture at the med school and the law school was so toxic. Classmates would tear pages out of research books in the library to get a competitive edge. Study groups were harder to crack into than secret societies. It was relentless. Ernie and I figured we'd do better together and rented a small apartment about

20 minutes away from the law school campus in Somerville. Now all we had to do was tell our parents. Over dinner during winter break, we decided it was time. He clinked his wine glass twice to get the table's attention.

"Debra and I have an announcement," he said in a booming voice as we both stood up from our seats. My father's eyes grew wide—I knew what he was thinking. Ernie's dad was a dentist, and his mother was a homemaker. They were a respectable family, and we were a good match.

"So we've decided to move in together," we announced to the table. "We'll save so much money living off campus, and we'll be able to study more without all the distraction of the dorms." We laid out every good reason for our decision, thinking we could cut our parents' concerns off at the pass. While we continued to explain ourselves, ticking off the checklist of all the answers to the questions we knew they'd have, my father sat up in his chair and fixed his eyes on me. He didn't say a word throughout our whole practiced speech. I knew the man well. He was clearly not happy. That's what prompted our trip to the sitting room for a chat. It was the longest 30-second walk of my life.

"You've just ruined your chances of ever being on the Supreme Court," my father said once we got out of earshot of the dining room. *Okay, that was not the reaction I was expecting.*

"Excuse me," I said with all the respect my confusion could muster. Being on the Supreme Court was not one of my life goals. I didn't even want to go to law school; that was my father's dream. Since I was a kid, he'd wax poetic about me being the first Black woman to sit on the highest court in the land, but I never actually thought he was serious. Turns out he was.

"How many couples do you think are living together at Harvard Law School?" he asked.

"Dad, I don't know. Maybe 60 to 70 percent," I guessed. He bristled at that number.

"I doubt that's true," my father said. "When you break up, it's always going to be your fault. Ernie can go do whatever he plans to do, but you? You won't just bounce back." I was flabbergasted. It was almost 1977. Did he really think my hopes and dreams would be determined by whether my boyfriend and I worked out? It sounded so ridiculous that I almost laughed. But I knew much better than to do that.

"I think we'll have to agree to disagree," I said gently as I watched my father's reaction with every word. Dad looked almost pained. I rarely stood up to him. Since I was a kid, I had always felt beholden to my dad's version of me. I was the youngest and, according to my sister Gretta, the reason my mother and father stayed together after a trial separation in 1965, right before my family moved to Greensboro. Even though I didn't know the details of their relationship then, I still felt like the glue keeping our family together. And a major part of that job meant keeping Dad, whose temper was legendary, happy. That meant being what he called "a good girl," getting good grades, looking the part of the perfectly poised young lady, never being too loud or rocking the boat too much.

I wasn't free. All my life I felt like I had to do what my dad told me. I was by far and away his favorite. But as I got older, the impossibly high pedestal he'd placed me on got more wobbly. Dad wanted me to go to an Ivy League school, so I did. He wanted me to be a lawyer, and I eventually went to law school. But that night at dinner, I just couldn't give up any more ground. I was tired of always being the peacemaker, of always trying to squeeze my own aspirations to fit into his vision instead of mine. Moving in with Ernie was a step toward independence.

Not to mention the fact that Dad was supporting me financially. That was another mighty hold he had on me. I could never truly rebel against him because he was the one mailing those tuition checks every semester. When he and Mom divorced in 1973, I couldn't take a side. If I did, it would have been my mother's. She'd always been our soft landing. She was the parent who gave goodnight kisses and said, "I love you." Delma L. Lee was the one who packed us up every few years without the faintest complaint whenever my dad came home with new station orders. "It'll be an adventure," she'd say with a smile when I complained about being the new kid yet again. She was a warm hug, my mother. Dad? Dad liked to push. But enough was enough. Ernie was a great guy—solid, dependable, ambitious, and supportive. I wouldn't give up our relationship because my father said so.

When we walked back to the dining room, Ernie made sure to catch my eye, raising his eyebrows with a silent question, *You okay?* I gave him a quick nod and sat down. My dad never supported our decision to move in together. But he dealt with it. He had grandiose plans for me, and as a kid it felt great to be believed in so fully. His confidence in me was unparalleled and was most certainly a key ingredient fueling my success. But as I grew into my own womanhood, that confidence felt more like control. I couldn't let him have this part of me too.

This was a time in my life when learning the difference between a push and a pull was critical, determining the path I'd take from Greensboro to Washington. Was I a lab mouse in a maze? Was I truly making my own choices, or was I being forced into decisions based on obstacles someone else placed in my way? It took time and a lot of perspective to recognize when I was being challenged versus when I was being controlled. And the tests started when I was at Brown.

The Ivy League wasn't on my radar at all in high school. As always it was my dad who kept pushing for it, even though North Carolina has excellent colleges and universities. In Greensboro, if you were brilliant and Black, the farthest you went was Duke University, about an hour away in Durham, or Howard University in Washington, DC. Practically no one went farther north, and rarer still was an Ivy League degree. But my father's word, as always, was law. Brown was my first choice because a group of students from the university traveling through the South had visited Dudley my senior year. Every single Black student in that group rocked the fluffiest and fullest afros I'd ever seen. I was sold. Dad nodded his head when my acceptance letter came as if it was already a foregone conclusion. My mother, who had no idea what the big deal was about the Ivy League, would've been just as happy if I'd gone down the street to North Carolina A&T.

I was pretty confident I could compete with the kids from Exeter and Choate, fancy boarding schools I'd never heard of before arriving in Providence with a trunk filled with sweaters my mother had knitted for me by hand. "It's going to be cold up there, Debi," she said while helping me pack. Okay, fine, I wasn't 100 percent confident that I could compete, but my dad's advice rang in my head: "Do the work." When my first papers came back—A's and B's across the board—I finally relaxed. *All right, I can do this.*

Somehow Dad had gotten a hold of a course catalog and plotted out two courses of study for me—for the next four years. "Your choice," said my father when he presented his—or should I say my—academic future. I managed to ignore it long enough to choose my own major. He hated that I decided to study Communist Chinese Ideology, of all subjects. "What on earth are you going to do with that?" he'd asked. It didn't seem practical or in line with his goal for me to sit on the Supreme Court some-day. "But," he said after thinking about it for a beat, "minoring in Chinese could be a smart business move." He reasoned that the country, which had been under communist rule for decades, was starting to open up its economy and American corporations would need employees who knew the lay of the land. "You're right, Dad," I said, leaning into the fiction that the whole thing was his idea all along.

By my junior year, I had enough credits to graduate a year early. But I decided to use that extra time to study abroad in Asia. As a political science major, I was interested in communist ide-ology as a possible path to equality for Black and brown peo-ple. Yes, yes, I know. Nerdy stuff. But that was the thing about Brown—being Black and a nerd were not mutually exclusive. You could—and in fact you were expected to—be both. The univer-sity taught us that there was nothing we couldn't do and nowhere we couldn't go. So why not China?

"China, huh?" said my academic advisor, Dean Verstandig, a man who like my father was inclined to push those he believed in toward greatness. "Well, the country is closed to foreigners right now." My face fell. I really wanted to go, not only to learn but because, if I was being honest with myself, having 7,000 miles between my dad and me didn't sound so bad.

"But," said Dean Verstandig, "I can get you close. How does Thailand sound?" I was on a plane the next semester. And Dad being Dad made sure to leave his mark on my trip. He somehow got me a position with Pertamina, the Indonesian national oil company. So while my fellow students were sleeping in monaster-ies and learning about microlending in the local market stalls, for my thesis research I traveled around the country on Pertamina's private jet, interviewing senior executives about the company's local community-building programs. Could a corporation really make a difference, or was it all just good PR? I had to answer that question while finishing up my thesis in Singapore. While I was in Southeast Asia during the fall of Saigon to the North Vietnamese Army, which marked the end of the decades-long Vietnam War, I got a phone call from my dad: "Don't give up your return ticket home!" The U.S. embassy had to abandon its embassy, and thousands of Americans in Saigon were being evacuated. My father didn't want me in that part of the world for one second longer than I had to be during such major political upheaval. So I never got to see China, but I did see myself in a new way. I was made of pretty tough stuff. The shy girl from Greensboro could hold her own thousands of miles away from home and in the middle of a war.

By the time I got back to the safety of College Hill, I wanted to dig even deeper into African American studies—something was itching at the back of mind about corporations and communities of color—but my dad forbade it.

"Don't you know who you are by now?" he asked.

He had a point. Who was I? What did I want to do? Who did I want to be? These are questions we rarely stop to ask ourselves as we're zooming from one accomplishment to the next, rarely giving ourselves a moment to breathe as we race to the next box that needs checking. Constantly needing to be in motion is what lands us in careers—in entire lives—that don't serve us or feed our souls. Chasing dreams that we've been told belong to us when really they don't. I was still trying to figure all that out, laying bare all the pieces of myself thus far to see how the puzzle fit together.

As the clock ticked down toward graduation, I knew I had a decision to make. I'd been a good student at Brown. I'd kept my head down and worked hard but was unsure of what my next move should be.

It was Dean Verstandig who told me I needed to apply to Harvard or Yale. I didn't want to go to either school. I was in his office in University Hall, an imposing structure that I hated having to go to for our academic meetings. The oldest building on campus, it always made me nervous; it felt like it could swallow you up whole.

"Your record's too good. You have to apply to at least one, Debra," he said. Yale had rejected my undergraduate application, and I was still holding a grudge about that. Harvard it was.

I cried the whole walk across the green and back to my room. If I applied to Harvard and got in, my dad would make me go. And deep down I knew I would get in. But would I fit in?

The Rhode Island School of Design was just down the hill, and I always imagined myself as one of those stylish kids who got to soak up art all day long. When I was growing up, my mother made all my clothes, and by college most of my wardrobe was filled with pieces I'd sewn myself—butterfly-collared blouses, halter jumpsuits, and flutter-sleeve dresses. Because although my father paid for school, he wasn't paying for anything else. When they divorced, my mother moved from our house in Benbow Park to a small one-bedroom her friend owned, supporting herself with her job at the white hospital. I remember once telling Mom that I didn't have enough money to do my laundry on the weekends, and a week later I got a check for $5 in the mail from her. She gave me whatever she had even when she didn't have much. I needed two jobs to support myself. So I worked at the library on campus and, my personal favorite, a clothing store called Arnold Palmer on Thayer Street where everyone shopped on College Hill.

Most days I'd go to morning classes, then head to my shift folding polos at the retail store, and then maybe split a plate of pancakes for dinner with my best friend Michele. Afterward I'd head home, hunched over a pile of course books studying well into the night instead of the beloved black-and-beige Singer sewing machine waiting for me back home in Greensboro.

Fashion designer had an exciting ring to it. But as always, my father had other plans. The heavy load of his dream deferred of being a lawyer all but crushed my own ambitions. The burden didn't make me angry so much as it made me feel invisible, slowly being made flat by a future I didn't want. My one small rebellion was to send in design school applications along with my law school applications, secretly praying for the former. But after doing my research, I found out that you needed more than Jesus and a personal essay to get into art school; you needed a portfolio of your work. I didn't have one aside from the clothes hanging in my closet. The introductory art class at Brown always filled up immediately, and semester after semester my name never came off the wait list. I couldn't get an admissions-worthy art portfolio together in time to be seriously considered. That was the end of that dream. Michele tried to cheer me up with a trip to IHOP, our favorite spot. "Maybe it's a sign, Debi. Maybe law school won't be so bad," she said. I doubted it. But I begrudgingly filled out my Harvard application anyway with a sinking feeling in my chest. My next rebellion was not telling my dad about it.

When my acceptance letter came that winter, I kept it to myself for a while. I'd fought the decision for so long that the joy I felt opening that fat envelope was almost surprising to me. I was proud of myself. Me. I'd done that. Despite the fact that law school was my dad's idea, I was the one who'd put in the work. This was my win, my decision. Because obviously I was going. Harvard is

Harvard. Only a fool would turn it down just to spite her father. I knew what the right decision was; I just didn't want Dad to think he'd made it for me. So I didn't rush to tell anyone, least of all him.

But word got out around my dorm. I had this one suitemate, Rachel, who had also applied to Harvard Law. When her envelope came, the news wasn't good, and almost immediately she flung her disappointment in my direction. "I can't believe Debi got in and I didn't," she said loud enough for me to hear. We were hardly friends. Black students stuck together like glue at Brown and rarely made time for anyone else. But this? The hostility. That was new. Brown prided itself on being the ivy with a heart. The school that didn't do hoity-toity. I rolled my eyes at Rachel before shooting back, "Affirmative action? Try all A's in political science, psych, and engineering." I hadn't stepped foot on Harvard's campus yet, and already things were changing. The knot in my stomach tightened even more.

Weeks went by before I called my dad with the news.

"But you didn't even apply to Harvard," responded my father, who was so involved in my law school application process that he knew Harvard hadn't been on *our* original list.

"Oh, well, Dean Verstandig suggested it at the last minute, and I decided to on a lark," I said.

"Umm-hmmm," harrumphed my dad. "I guess I'll be sending checks to Boston next year."

My mom's reaction was priceless.

"Oh, congratulations, Debi. That's just wonderful, honey. Now where is Harvard?"

It was only an hour and a half north on the I-95, but I nearly didn't make it to Boston that fall. Long story short, a boy (almost) got in the way.

I wanted to call this chapter in my life "A Funny Thing

Happened on the Way to Law School," but there was nothing funny about my traumatic transition from Brown to Harvard. I was so focused on prepping for law school that I didn't make any plans for my summer in Providence after graduation. All I knew for sure was that I didn't want to move home to my mother's tiny apartment in Greensboro. My friends Michele and Marsha had rented an apartment on the top floor of a beautiful old Victorian on College Hill. They wanted me to be their third, but I didn't have enough money saved to cover the rent. My sister, Gretta, came to my rescue.

"I think I know of something," she said when I called her in a panic. Gretta had a glamorous job working in fashion at the flagship Bloomingdale's in Manhattan. With her contacts in the retail business, my ever-resourceful big sister found me a job doing administration work at a local jewelry factory in Providence. She wanted me to have one last hurrah with my girlfriends before we all scattered across the country chasing our respective bright futures. Me to law school. Michele to a master's in public health at the University of Michigan. What Gretta didn't know was that there was another reason I really wanted to stay in Providence, and it had nothing to do with my pals. His name was Isaac, and we'd been friends all throughout college. Best friends actually. "You two should just go on ahead and date," Michele always teased when the three of us would be out together. Something or someone always got in the way though. Me going to Thailand. Isaac being busy with class. Both of us not wanting to ruin the friendship. But by June of 1976 it was clear that something was brewing. Isaac, who'd always been content to hang with the girls and me, started to invite me and only me over to his place to "relax." Michele and Marsha would *ooohhh* and *ahhhh* as I headed out the door. One such night changed everything.

Congresswoman Barbara Jordan, the first Southern Black woman to be elected to Congress, was going to be the first Black woman to deliver the DNC's keynote address. "We have to watch together, Debi," said Isaac when he called our apartment earlier that day to invite me over to his place. This was the original Netflix and chill. "Très romantique!" joked Michele. "Be still my heart," cried Marsha. That's what I loved about Isaac though; he never tried too hard around me. He wasn't like the other guys at Brown, constantly angling for something more. Isaac was a true friend who liked debating politics and policy with me.

The two of us sat together on Isaac's comfy bed watching the Democratic National Convention on his 13-inch black-and-white TV. It was a historic night. When Congresswoman Jordan said, "We are a people in a quandary about the present. We are a people in search of our future," she might as well have been speaking directly to me. I was still so nervous about Harvard, about the life laid out in front of me, about how I could shape it, and then Congresswoman Jordan offered some words of wisdom. "As a first step," she said while conceptualizing the American dream, "we must restore our belief in ourselves." I started to relax for the first time since getting my acceptance letter. I stayed over that night, and Isaac and I slept together for the first (and last) time. Summer was feeling a little lighter, but weeks later the consequences of that night crashed through my carefully laid plans like a wrecking ball.

I was on my way to the break room for lunch when I reached into my desk's bottom drawer for the leftovers I'd placed there that morning. That's when I noticed the tampons I kept stashed away, still there. How long had it been? I counted back in my head to my last period, and the dread began to creep in. "I'm sure you're fine," Michele said that night when I told her my worst fear. Two days later a doctor at the women's clinic near campus confirmed it, and I couldn't hold back my tears.

When I called Isaac to tell him the news, I could barely get past the sentence "I'm pregnant. What are we—" before he hung up on me.

He didn't want to hear the rest or stand by me for the next decision. I held the receiver in my hand stunned but determined. Calling him back, begging for Isaac's help, wasn't going to make things better. I already knew what I wanted to do. There was zero doubt in my mind. This wasn't my baby. But my self-assurance didn't make Isaac's reaction any less painful. Just because I could do this on my own didn't mean I wanted to. If instead of hanging up on me he had said, "I love you, Debs," perhaps my life would have taken a sharp left turn that Friday afternoon. Or at the very least I would have taken longer to come to the decision I knew was imminent. Instead, the faintest possibility of becoming a mother disappeared with the empty hum of the dial tone.

My next call was to Gretta, who had been my role model my entire life. Growing up, sometimes she seemed more like a second mother to me than a big sister, disciplining me whenever I got out of line. But when I was at Brown, our relationship transitioned into something new. The more time we spent together in New York—two young women exploring the big city hand in hand—the more we became actual friends.

"Don't worry, Debi," she reassured me. "We'll take care of it. I love you."

Roe v. Wade, the landmark Supreme Court decision that made abortion legal nationwide, had been passed just three years earlier in 1973. I'd always supported a woman's right to choose, I just didn't think I'd need to choose so soon. Gretta wasted no time making the appointment, and a few weeks later there I was at the Providence Amtrak station waiting for my life to go back to normal.

The train platform was completely empty as I counted down the minutes for the regional to New York to arrive. I felt like my feet were stuck to the cement. I kept looking over my shoulder, still hoping that Isaac, who'd been my friend for years, might show up to hold my hand through all of this. "All aboard," shouted one of the conductors as I began climbing the steps onto the train. I held on to the railing and took one last glance at the platform. Isaac never showed. We didn't speak again until decades later. On the Amtrak barreling toward Manhattan and my sister and the solution to this problem, I said to no one but myself, "This is not how my story ends." A baby, Isaac, Harvard? The choice was clear. I was going to go on with the rest of my life, *mine*. That's the life I was choosing. I wasn't going to let one misstep derail everything.

The pregnancy was like a tidal wave, threatening to drown and destroy everything I'd built in my life thus far. I had this great opportunity. I was on my way to the best law school in the country. Everyone, and I mean everyone, was happy. I was a hero at Brown, a hero back in Greensboro. Everything was going right. All I had to do was pack. And then this.

Grieving wasn't really an option. I had less than a month before orientation in Cambridge. Which meant I had just enough time to go to New York and get the procedure, head back to Greensboro to say goodbye to my mother, return to my apartment in Providence to pack up the rest of my things, and then make my way to Cambridge to start my first year in one of the most competitive law programs in the country. It was a whirlwind, and I had tunnel vision, so focused on pushing forward to prove to myself that my admission was not a mistake that I didn't give myself a moment of air. Sometimes you have to put one foot in front of the other and keep going. I locked up the natural sadness and guilt I felt and packed them away, buried them somewhere far away. Because if I didn't, they would pull me down, and I couldn't let myself be dragged into the deep, not now when everything else in my life was headed up. I had a road map to follow. I had to focus on law school and set my sights on that goal. I was stronger than I thought I was.

More importantly, I knew how fragile my future was as a Black woman in America. Yes, I was smart. I was educated. I was driven. But one wrong turn could ruin everything I'd been working toward—which was what exactly? Again at 21, I wasn't entirely sure. But I knew having a baby with a guy who couldn't be bothered to pick up the phone definitely was not it. I never regretted my decision, even though I told no one except for Gretta, Michele, and Ernie, the guy who comforted me when his friend wouldn't and who would later become my first grown-up love.

When I lugged my trunk into my new dorm room for the first time, I was greeted by a sobbing white girl on one of the twin beds.

"Um, hi," I said. "I'm Debra. And you are?"

"J-J-Jill," she said in between moans. "I'm so sorry. I'm not usually like this." Jill was one of the fancy boarding school graduates I had been nervous about competing against when I first arrived on Brown's campus what seemed like a lifetime before.

"What's wrong?" I asked her as I set my trunk down at the foot of my bed.

"It's my boyfriend," she said, and I braced myself. Men. They ruined everything. "He's at Yale School of Architecture and I just miss him so, so much," she said, breaking down again. Was this girl serious? She was hyperventilating in front of a stranger because her college sweetheart was a two-hour drive away? I wanted to roll my eyes.

"Oh, that's too bad," I said, before hightailing it out of there. I had just had an abortion and had been forced to pack every emotion surrounding it out of sight. But this girl? She missed her boyfriend. I could swim in the gallons of tears Jill cried that first month over her sweet Bradley. But me, I just soldiered on, sometimes smoothing my hands over my stomach and imagining what would have been. Then quickly banishing all those thoughts from my head as I buried my nose into a Civil Procedure book as thick as the Bible. On that first day, confronted with Jill's sobs, I almost gave myself over to my own pain. But instead, I dialed a number I had saved in my address book of the only other person I sort of knew in Cambridge.

"Hi, um, it's Debra. From Brown?" I said by way of reintroduction.

"Of course. How are they treating you at HLS?" asked Ernie in a bright voice that would come to make my days. He sounded like he really wanted to know, and I felt myself wanting to tell him.

"Okay, I guess. It's just a lot. I wish I knew more people here."

"You know me," said Ernie, feigning hurt. "Where'd you end up? In Hastings, I bet."

"How'd you know?"

"It's got the biggest rooms—and it's closest to the law library," he said. We both laughed. "Hey," Ernie ventured. "Be downstairs in 15."

That first September in Boston belonged to Ernie. If we had free time, which wasn't often, then we spent it in each other's company. It felt easy. Ernie was the quiet pause I'd been denying myself since I found out I was pregnant months before. It was as if I'd been sprinting from mile to mile in a never-ending marathon and Ernie was the one who laid a hand on my shoulder to say, "Slow down." All we did was walk and talk and talk and talk. But we never discussed what had happened between Isaac and me. We did not talk about the abortion. But Ernie knew whatever happened in Providence that summer had been bad, really bad. I didn't ask him to choose a side, but he did. The first time he reached for my hand on one of our walks, I knew. We were inseparable.

Choice is a privilege. From the really big things, like what women are *allowed* to do with their bodies, to the seemingly small moments, like how we style our hair, the ability to decide whether to turn right or left is a freedom too many of us take for granted. I know I did. Actually, no, that's not quite right. I understood that choice wasn't just a privilege but the root of true power and self-determination. What I didn't know was how to exercise the authority I had over my own life. Until I did. My father had succeeded in making so many big life decisions for me—where I went to school, what I studied, and, when it came to Ernie, whom I shared my life with. And for years I chafed against the strong hold Dad had over me. But that summer between Brown and Harvard changed me. I realized then that I was much stronger than I thought I was. I wish I didn't have to be. I wish I didn't have to make the choices I was forced to make. But in the end, I was proud of myself for owning it, for choosing me.

I was proud of the choice I'd made and thankful I had the right to make it. It was one of the first times in my life when I was solely responsible for what happened next. No one else would seal my fate—not my dad, an admissions officer, or that jealous white suitemate who assumed I'd only gotten into Harvard because of affirmative action. It was a powerful moment in life that solidi-fied a fundamental philosophy that would stay with me always: Whatever you do, own it. Because the consequences—good or bad—are yours and yours alone.

CHAPTER FOUR

GETTING THROUGH THE GAUNTLET

I've never had a female mentor. Let that sink in. Throughout my entire professional life—from Harvard Law to a coveted federal clerkship and then Big Law—the people who shaped my career were men, always men. Never once did I have a woman to follow, ask advice from, or simply vent to.

Instead, there were the men who pushed and prodded me onto paths I either was unsure of or downright didn't want to step foot on. But there they were, urging me forward with "You *have* to do this" and "No one would turn that down, Debra." It wasn't until I met Bob Johnson, someone who encouraged more than he demanded, that I ever saw not just a well-trodden road before me but alternative routes to the same destination. He showed me that I could follow my own passion, switching gears and lanes without someone else's instructions guiding each turn. BET was like open road. It was freedom. But to get there, first I had to navigate myself out of a winding gauntlet of opinionated men.

Of course, it all started with Dad, who'd mapped out my life from the womb—law school, law firm, and then the Supreme Court. Easy. But even after I achieved *his* ultimate dream of getting into Harvard Law, there were still more powerful male voices to contend with.

"Lee!" barked Professor Ferguson from his wooden lectern. This was week one, day three. I'd barely sat down to crack open my Civil Procedure textbook before my name rang out, ricocheting against the walls of the lecture hall like an alarm bell. All 140 pairs of eyes in the room zeroed in on me. I shrank inside, silently praying that there was another Lee somewhere in that room.

"Lee! Debra L.," he repeated, even louder if that was possible. There was no mistaking it this time. Out of all these eager faces in the crowd, why on earth was he calling on me?

"Uh, yes," I managed to stammer before Professor Ferguson began grilling me relentlessly on a case that laid the foundation of civil procedure for the next 10 minutes. *What was at the heart of the case? What was the precedent set? How did it affect corporate litigation moving forward?* I managed to eke out a few barely acceptable answers, having read a bit about the case before class. "Humph," he mumbled by way of reply before I was allowed to sit back down, almost certain my time at Harvard was over before it had begun. Was this what law school was going to be like? Angry older men shouting questions at you in front of a mass of students who are all too happy to watch you fail in public?

"You sure you're okay?" asked Ernie later that day when I told him what had happened, how I ran to the bathroom after class and cried hot tears as I realized my mistake in thinking law school was for me. How, after I left, an upperclassman TA found me looking dazed and confused and tried to offer some words of encouragement. "Don't worry," she said. "You'll do better next time."

"What?" I said horrified. The only thing that had gotten me out of the bathroom was the knowledge that at least I'd gotten my humiliation over with during an early class and had a few months to prepare for the next public flogging. "What do you mean 'next time'?"

"Oh, he's coming back to you. That's your case now. He's going to call on you all year," she said with a sly grin as I crumbled inside. *I'm never ever going to make it.* There was no way I could go through that again. Ernie tried to cheer me up, but I was certain Professor Ferguson's master plan was to get me to quit law school altogether. Because the way he picked on me in Civil Procedure had me on the verge of packing up my books and heading home. I swear he didn't want me to be a lawyer. He couldn't have. He'd seen through my *fake it till you make it* act. He knew I didn't really want to be there. And he was offering me an easy out by tormenting me once a week.

What made it worse was that Professor Ferguson was Black and I was one of the few Black women in his class. The goal was to make me twice as good, and in his view the deep end was the best place to start if you wanted to swim with the sharks. Clarence Clyde Ferguson was an army vet, a former ambassador to Uganda, and a famed legal scholar who himself had graduated from Harvard Law in 1951. The man did not play. Entering his lecture hall once a week was like walking through water. I had to force every step to my wooden seat, willing myself to breathe because I knew what was coming. The stress of it made me sick to my stomach.

"Debra!" he'd bark.

In his mind he was helping me. The Socratic Method is the foundation of a legal education. Instead of rote memorization, law students are expected to participate in rigorous discussions in order to train their minds to analyze the facts of a case like a lawyer. Participation was life. But Black law students often didn't get called on during lectures, even when their hands were eagerly waving in the air. That implicit bias was apparent to anyone paying attention, and Professor Ferguson saw it as his duty as a Black academic to right that wrong in his classroom. I completely understood that—in theory. But this was me we're talking about. Speaking up was never my strong suit. I thrived on research and could recall all the relevant facts when given the time. I liked diving deep into the text, taking meticulous notes, and testing. That's what got me through Brown. But Harvard Law was not the safe space that Brown had been.

Cold calls—when professors yelled your name to answer a legal question with zero prep—were my kryptonite. Professor Ferguson thought drilling me in front of the class every week would draw me out of my shell and make me a better litigator because that's just the way things were done in law school. But I didn't want to be a lawyer, much less a trial lawyer. By putting me on the spot, he assumed he was including me in the process since most white professors, which is to say most professors, wouldn't call on women or people of color; they just looked past your raised hand. But instead of training me to think on my feet, his razor-sharp attention cut me to shreds. After each interaction, I just felt weaker and less prepared for life as a lawyer. Who could shine in that kind of environment?

That class was a hard lesson in grinning and bearing it. Trust me, reciting more facts and analysis about "my case" each week did not make me love the law any more or hate speaking up in front of class any less. But giving up was not an option. My father had made it plain that the only postgraduate education he was willing to pay for was law school. So instead of packing up my books and hightailing it back to Greensboro, I tacked on another year of school at Harvard by getting a master's in public policy from the John F. Kennedy School of Government. If I was going to be forced to play the game and play by someone else's rules, then I would have to make the win worth it for me. Policy was always my first love. I'd gone to Brown to study political science with dreams of being a journalist, helping write the first draft of history and the seismic changes in the world I'd witnessed as a young girl in the segregated South. Instead of letting law school derail that dream completely, I would bend the experience, which I knew I was privileged to have, to fit into my vision for my future, not anyone else's.

I got my first-ever C in Ferguson's course and accepted it as a badge of honor. He taught me that I could survive anything if I could see a bigger goal within reach. That experience would come in handy more times than I could count when I began climbing the corporate ladder. I knew back then that I would never be one of those courtroom attorneys you see on TV cross-examining witnesses and swaying a stone-faced jury with an enthusiastic closing argument—Civil Procedure made sure of that. But I did learn something—not all mentors come in the package you'd expect. They don't all encourage with kind words and a shoulder to cry on. Some of the best teach you what to steer clear of as opposed to what to run toward. That was the lesson that would carry me through my first job out of law school.

With my dual degrees from Harvard in law and policy, my plan was to work in the government. I saw myself in the White

House one day advising presidents. (I would get there eventually, but not in the role I imagined.) The Securities and Exchange Commission had hired me in its policy department. Ernie and I were on our way to Washington. We'd gotten married right before our last year at Harvard in 1979. Ours was a big Southern affair with hundreds of folks from both sides convening in Greensboro for the wedding. Dad thought we were too young, but since we were already living together, he was content with the fact that we were making it official. My mother was over the moon. Really, it was her wedding.

"So, Debi, what do you think about—?" she'd call to ask me in between classes.

"Whatever you want, Mom," I'd cut in, too busy gearing up for finals to plan a wedding. Ernie and I arrived in my hometown that weekend in August for the ceremony, spent a week honeymooning in Bermuda, and then got back to Boston to finish our final year of school. I was 24, and the marriage was one of the first completely independent decisions I'd made up until then.

Ernie had been matched in the pediatrics department at Children's National Hospital in Washington, and I was on my way to the government. It seemed like a perfect setup. But then yet another mentor convinced me to go a different direction.

The SEC had one of the best policy offices in the federal government, so when I got an offer from the agency, I was beyond excited. Finally, I'd get to go my own way. This was my chance to put my passion and purpose to good use. But a judge I had clerked for in Salem, Massachusetts, during law school thought I was being too hasty in giving up the law side of my education, and he suggested I do a federal clerkship in Washington for at least a year. He had just the man in mind—Barrington Parker Sr., a federal judge of the United States District Court in DC and a Republican.

"But, Judge," I said, "you know I really don't want to be a lawyer." My mentor was undeterred.

"You can't turn down a federal clerkship, Debra. And after a year, you can go to the SEC. But use your law degree," he told me. And I listened despite my better judgment. My gut kept telling me to go with my first mind. Head to the SEC and never look back. But everyone—my law school professors, my classmates, my dad—kept repeating the same line: "You can't turn this down. Folks would kill for this opportunity, Debra."

Judge Parker was a hard man. Actually, hard doesn't quite cut it. The man was tough as nails, all iron and steel. He'd lost his left leg when a car struck him as he was crossing the street to buy a pack of cigarettes, but he didn't let his metal crutches slow him down for one second. The sound of the judge's crutches clicking and clacking against the floor was terrifying to his clerks. Supreme Court Justice Thurgood Marshall's son, Thurgood Marshall Jr., who we all called Goody, clerked for Parker with me, and he was a notorious practical jokester. Goody would walk past my desk near the elevators and jingle his keys to make me think the judge was on his way. Then he'd poke his head around my desk and cackle. "Gotcha, Debi!" he'd say when he saw me furiously typing, trying to look busy. "Goody!"

Much like Professor Ferguson, Judge Parker, a Black man who'd grown up in DC, saw his courtroom as a battlefield and treated his chambers like boot camp, grilling us like a law professor would. He thought that style was the only way to make us tougher, better. But it nearly broke me down, making me more anxious than capable. I was the judge's first Black female clerk, and he made it his mission to prepare me for the rigors of a career in the courtroom. He thought of me like a daughter and a new recruit all in one. In his chambers, he was the general, and our job was to fall in line. You'd walk into his office preparing for war.

"Debra, what did I say three drafts ago?" he asked me during one of my first weeks on the job. Three drafts ago? I had no idea. I'd barely been there three days. "Who wrote that opinion?" I looked around to my fellow clerks hoping they'd help me out, but no such luck.

"Uh, I'm not sure."

"Go and find out," he barked.

"Okay," I said, ready to turn on my heels and run.

"What did you say?" asked Judge Parker.

"Okay?" I ventured, not sure what he meant.

"Try again," he said. That's when one of my fellow clerks finally took pity on me and whispered just loud enough in my direction, "Yes, sir."

"Yes, sir," I repeated aloud. Judge Parker nodded and waved me out of the room.

One of the judge's highest-profile cases was the criminal trial of John Hinkley Jr., the man who, on March 30, 1981, shot and wounded President Ronald Reagan outside the Hilton on Connecticut Avenue in Washington. As the lowly third clerk in the judge's chambers, it was my job to show up to the courtroom before everyone else and fill the ice-water pitchers at the bench, the plaintiff's table, and the defendant's table. I remember arriving early one Monday and doing my rounds, grabbing the metal pitchers from the courthouse kitchen and putting them in place.

As I walked out of the courtroom toward the elevator to chambers, I passed three police officers with their bomb-sniffing dogs going in after me.

"This isn't right! I'm over there risking my life getting inside before the bomb-sniffing dogs," I complained to Ernie later that night. He was listening but just barely, exhausted as he was from being on call at the hospital the day before. We were struggling to get our footing not only as young professionals but as a young married couple.

Our first year in DC was drudgery. Ernie and I lived in a duplex on Capitol Hill, and at 7 a.m. we'd kiss each other goodbye; he'd head in one direction to his internship at the hospital, and I'd head in the other direction toward the courthouse for another day of mental torture in Judge Parker's chambers. My husband was dealing with life and death, and I was more nervous about going to work than he was. Adding to all that stress, all my free time was spent studying for the bar that summer.

When I found out I failed by just a few points, my heart sank. All I could think was, *What's the judge going to say?*

I walked to chambers with lead in my heels, willing myself to take each step. None of us liked going in there. It was a huge, traditional room with dark-wood paneling on the wall and a massive mahogany desk with a giant black-leather wingback chair for the judge. It felt like the place could blot you out. I knocked gingerly, hoping he wouldn't hear me and I could head back to my desk near the elevators without a word. But no such luck. "Enter!" he snapped from the behind the closed door.

"Yes?" he said without looking up from the mountain of opinions, cases, and evidence that seemed to live permanently on that massive desk of his.

"Well," I ventured, unsure of how to spit it out. "The thing is," I continued, my voice quivering. If there was one thing Judge Parker did not abide, it was a shaky voice.

"Debra," he said, finally looking up and into my eyes, which at this point were on the verge of flooding.

"I failed the bar," I spit out in one breath to get it over with before I started crying in front of this man, but it was too late for that. I was crying.

"Oh, no," he said with a soft tone I had never once heard before. "Come around here and take my hand," said Judge Parker. I did just that. "Don't worry about this. You will have many failures in your life. This is the first of several, and you'll keep going."

Was this the same man who'd shouted at me to keep better track of my work just the day before? The man who made sure we typed all of our drafts before handing them to his secretary to retype? The man who terrified us all so much that we sat up straighter when the elevator doors dinged and we heard his metal crutches clanging on the floor?

"You'll be okay, Debra," he continued. "This will make you stronger."

A part of me wanted to believe him. And in the end, he was right. The entire experience of working with Judge Parker had made me stronger. He'd toughened me up to the point that no job since has ever been as hard. He helped me uncover my grit. So much so that I knew I couldn't take the bar again. I found out that you could appeal your essay score by defending your bluebook answers with additional written arguments. Unsurprisingly, Dad was none too happy when he found out I hadn't passed with flying colors the first time. Mom, of course, was a lot more understanding and wished me luck on my appeal so no pressure at all. I was a ball of nerves the afternoon I took my appeal test. I don't think I let myself really breathe until my new results came: I passed.

After my year of clerking was up, I was ready to flee to the nearest exit. Judge Parker wanted me to stay on another year, but I knew I wouldn't survive it. The SEC had put my policy job on hold but by the time I was ready to start Ronald Reagan was president and had put a hiring freeze on all federal jobs. Besides, I didn't want to work for a Republican administration. Despite my repeated insistence that I didn't want to be a lawyer, I figured joining a law firm until the Democrats returned to power was the smarter move. It took them 12 years.

My plan was to hide out at a firm for a few years and then go back to policy work, my first love. But the Republicans kept winning. Again, I tried to find a way to marry the path I was on with my vision for future. Unlike some of the fancy New York firms, Steptoe and Johnson in DC was always known as the firm with a heart. It treated its associates well and had an active pro bono program where you could work on cases you cared about. Plus, at the time, Steptoe had an unheard-of number of Black attorneys—10 associates and two partners—which was nearly three times as many as any other corporate law firm in the city. Everything pointed to Steptoe. If I was going to be forced into the law, it seemed like the obvious choice. Not to mention that my starting salary was $42,000 more than I'd thought I'd ever make in life.

But firm life wasn't for me. The cases, the hours, the culture, the people. Nothing about Big Law felt right.

"Well, if it was supposed to be fun," said Dad when I told him the truth about what life was like as an associate at a law firm, "then they wouldn't call it work now, would they, Debra?"

First let's start with the work. Steptoe knew my interest lay in regulatory work, since that was closest to my love of policy, so the firm put me to work for one of its biggest clients: the Atlantic Richfield Company, a big oil corporation. As an associate, your job is research. For months and months, I woke up at dawn to get to the office before everyone else and spend the next 8 to 10 hours in the law library reading about oil and gas regulations. God, it was boring—and isolating. My office was situated in between two of the firm's most powerful partners, so all my fellow associates were too afraid to stop by for any reason other than to drop off paperwork and run. It was a lonely existence. Seven days a week—yes, seven, because at a big firm you were expected to bill weekend hours too—I had my head in a book or bent over a typewriter writing yet another memo about the Federal Energy Regulatory Commission's latest rules. Unhappy didn't cover it. I was miserable.

"Debra, where are you going?" asked Ernie from the front door of the posh Dupont Circle townhouse we'd moved to on our new salaries. It was 5 a.m., and he was just getting home after being on call at Children's for the previous 24 hours. I was already in my boring gray pantsuit and headed out the door.

"I have to get to the office."

"Now?"

"Yes now!" I'd found a typo in a memo I'd finished the night before. I had to get to the office, fix it on my massive IBM Selectric typewriter, and replace it before the partner who expected to read it that morning found out.

I grabbed my trench coat and pushed past Ernie, not even bothering to say goodbye. We'd been two ships passing in the night for the better part of our brief time in DC, and at 25 and 26 neither one of us knew how to fix the growing tension. For both of us, work was taking precedence over our young marriage. The issue wasn't love. We had plenty between us. It just wasn't enough to sail through the fog. Ernie and I divorced amicably after two years as husband and wife.

"It's okay, Debi," my mother said when I called her with the news, knowing that she would be the parent to provide comfort instead of criticism. She and my father had been divorced for nearly a decade by then, and she'd picked herself up and started over without complaint. Dad was hard, but my mother was the real rock of our family. I also remembered Judge Parker's advice when I told him I'd failed the bar: "You will have many failures in your life. This is the first of several, and you'll keep going."

For the next few years, I plunged into work at Steptoe, hoping the long hours would eventually add up to something greater. But it wasn't helping. I still couldn't get my footing there no matter how much I tried to make Big Law culture bend to my will— taking on pro bono work, recruiting Black law students, mentoring first-year associates. None of it made the time commitment, mind-numbing cases, and corporate greed worth it to me. I never felt like myself when I walked through the glass doors of our downtown offices. I needed a new mentor, preferably one who was Black and a woman, but I would settle for checking at least one of those boxes.

A mentor is someone who advises you, takes the time to get to know you, and helps you navigate the politics of the office and the intricacies of your field. They can tell you where the pitfalls are and which roadblocks to avoid. They are invaluable and provide immeasurable guidance, especially when you are new. I finally found one in Tyrone Brown.

Ty was a former commissioner of the Federal Communications Commission, which regulates communications by radio, television, wire, satellite, and this newfangled thing called cable. Communications law, especially with the wide new frontier of cable, was where I really got excited. The work was infinitely more interesting and less morally ambiguous than corporate oil and gas. During my third and fourth years at the firm, Ty, who was Black, started to take me under his wing. He particularly needed help with one of his smaller clients, a fledgling cable channel called BET. It was a new media company based in Washington, not New York, which was not only rare but meant that Steptoe could be at the forefront of cutting-edge development. As a bonus, it was owned and operated by a Black man.

Sure, Steptoe had more Black lawyers than any of the other firms downtown. But racism still existed inside the building or for our clients. I'd experienced it firsthand myself.

I was on a conference call with a partner at the firm, Jim McHugh, and one of our communications clients, a West Virginia media company. My job was to explain to the company's owner why its FCC licensing wasn't being fast-tracked.

"None of those preferences apply to you, unfortunately," I explained to our client, which was at the beginning stages of the TV and radio licensing process. Minority-owned businesses usually got priority, since those types of businesses were few and far between. The playing field was anything but level, so minority businesses received preferences. Without standing on that soapbox, I was politely explaining to our client, a business owned and operated by white men, that they had no special dispensation when one of the company's executives decided to make a "joke."

"So our name won't get us to the front of the line," he said with a laugh.

The company was named I c n .

It took me a minute to re l x i h w y Jane of

us could see one another on the conference call, and I had never met with this client in person. There was silence as the punch line landed with a heavy thud. Shocked, I had no clue what to say. Jim McHugh, the Steptoe partner on this case, was quicker.

"No," he said. "That won't get you any preference, nor will the fact that one of your attorneys is a Black woman." There was more silence on the line before the owner apologized and I moved on to the next item on our agenda. When the meeting was over, Jim personally apologized to me for our client's behavior. "He was so out of line," Jim said. I appreciated it, but it shouldn't have been necessary. The incident was a stark reminder that when you're not in the room, you never know what's being said. It was also another mark against life at the firm.

I went to Ty, my mentor, and asked for more BET work.

"Let's get you and Bob together," he said.

My first job was getting acquainted with the "must carry" rules, which stated that a cable operator had to carry all the locally broadcast TV stations in its market before it carried any additional specialty satellite cable channels like BET. The FCC's goal with the rule was to ensure that smaller broadcast channels weren't left behind in the new wild west of cable superstations. Media mogul Ted Turner, who then ran WTBS and CNN out of Atlanta, sued the FCC over the "must carry" rule on the grounds that it violated his First Amendment rights. Bob Johnson wanted to support Turner's lawsuit by filing an amicus brief, also known as a "friend of the court" brief, to show that the ruling impacted other unique cable networks with niche markets like BET.

But first I had to figure out what cable TV was and how it worked.

"Go meet with Bob," Ty told me. "He'll explain."

I walked into BET's swanky office in Georgetown and was

immediately impressed. As a former Hill staffer turned lobby-ist, the space was right up Bob's alley—all sleek glass, buzzing with energy, and filled with impeccably dressed Black executives. This place was nothing like Steptoe, which felt stuffy and formal. In the lobby, I passed more Black people in the time it took me to walk to the reception area than I did all day working at the firm. "I'm here to see Bob," I told the receptionist, who looked me over—in my navy suit with the white bow—and gave me a slight approving nod before pointing me down the hall that led to Bob's office. It felt like going to see the Great Oz. But when I knocked on the door, Bob was all smiles.

"Ah, Debra. I've been expecting you," he said as he directed me to the leather chair opposite his desk.

"Am I late?" I asked as I eased into my seat and pulled out a legal pad, ready to take notes.

"Not at all," said Bob with a bright grin before leaning against his desk and getting down to brass tacks. "Shall we get started?" And then for the next hour, Bob Johnson, the CEO of Black Entertainment Television, took the time to break down the cable business to a young lawyer he'd just met. Like no professor or mentor I'd ever known before, no question was too small, no concept too big that he couldn't at least try to explain it to a novice. Pulling out a white pad and a pen from his desk, Bob drew a triangular satellite dish in the far right corner. Then a fat round circle for Earth in the middle. He added arrows beaming programming to and from the satellite and the planet. That's how I learned about cable. I wasn't just impressed, I was appreciative. Here was the CEO of a company doing what so many of the other influencers in my career previously hadn't—he took the time.

"If 'must carry' laws continue," he explained, "then emerging cable networks like BET would get kicked off the system. If an operator can only carry 25 stations and gets bogged down with every local broadcast channel from kingdom come, then BET would be the 26th channel, and no one would see us."

I spent an hour and a half with Bob that afternoon, getting a master class in cable and his plans for BET, which we still couldn't even get in Washington. When I walked back to Steptoe to write the amicus brief, I felt a shift. What Bob was doing at BET was important and necessary, and I wanted to be a part of it. Working with Ty on BET was my first meaningful project at the firm in all four years I'd been there. It felt personal even though I couldn't go home and turn on the channel. That was my next project: applying to get a cable franchise licensed in DC so that folks in the city could actually watch one of the only networks based in the nation's capital. Every time Ty poked his head into my office, I got excited, knowing that another BET assignment was coming.

This was another crossroads moment for me. I'd gotten the Ivy League education and the law degree and "made it." But I knew where my heart was, and it wasn't at the firm. I wanted to work for a media company. Leaping to something new when you've worked so hard to achieve what you have isn't just terrifying, it seems like a betrayal. All the money my dad spent on my education, all the sleepless and stress-filled nights I spent in the law library trying to make it through Harvard. What did they add up to if not the distinguished career I had and should've been grateful for? Would I be throwing it all away if I decided to leave the firm and work as in-house counsel at a media company? I was still on the fence. But as often happens, outside forces pushed me.

As a fifth-year associate, it was time to set my sights on the partner track (and languish unfulfilled for the rest of my law career). Sure, I disliked the firm—I had no illusions about that—but I'd also put in five years of my life. My reviews were always excellent. My colleagues liked collaborating with me, and my work spoke for itself. I'd also helped Ty Brown immensely when it came to his top client, BET. But at the annual partner meeting that year, when the big guys threw around the names they thought should be in the running to join them, mine wasn't mentioned in the room.

"Ty, what happened? Did anyone push for me?" I asked after the news came down later that week announcing the career-defining promotion. My name never came up. Despite not even wanting it, I was still hurt and mostly confused.

Ty told me matter-of-factly that he was not sure what happened. He suggested that if I wanted to become a partner that I back off BET work and ask some of the oil and gas lawyers, those with more influence, if they needed help with their client list. Turns out despite having great mentors who provided me with new knowledge of the industry, no one was in a position to push me through to partner. Good advice is one thing, a great thing. Mentors are necessary for that reason alone. But you can't stop there if you want to truly climb the ladder in your field. You must also have a sponsor. They can speak your name in halls of power, making sure it echoes in all the right corners. I didn't have a sponsor, and I didn't even know it. I'd just assumed those two roles were one in the same.

This was a clear sign that I had to leave Steptoe and Johnson. There was no place for me there, especially if doing the work I loved most was getting me nowhere. So I started interviewing with big media companies in New York—HBO and CBS Records—to join their in-house legal teams. But every time I got back to Washington from Manhattan, I felt my body physically relax as the Amtrak pulled into Union Station. New York was certainly exciting but DC had become home. BET felt that way too. Bob seemed to agree.

Ty, Bob, and I were at a hearing on the cable franchise at the DC City Council. We had a midday break, and Ty had to head back to the office to wrap up another project.

Bob turned to me and asked, "Would you like to have lunch, Debra?" I nodded, none too eager to head back to the firm. We went to a restaurant across the street from city hall and Bob, as usual, wasted no time.

"Why don't you come over to BET and be our general counsel?"

Behind the scenes, the network had a legal issue that could become complicated. BET had signed a contract that it wanted to get out of but legally couldn't. It'd hired a production company to produce a show called *Life and Times of the Black Rich and Famous*, and instead, it got something more like *The Fuzzy Footage of a Few Folks with Some Money*. It was a mess. The production quality was unbearably low. Bob and his programming head hated it. Thing is, they hadn't read the deal before they signed it, and there was no quality control clause in the contract. Bob was new to original programming deals. The network was still in its infancy and relied heavily on reruns of old Black movies and music videos. Original programming was the dream, but the nuts and bolts weren't in place yet.

Inside I was doing cartwheels. General counsel? I was just six years out of law school. General counsel was the epitome of a lawyer's career outside of making partner in Big Law. This man I'd known for all of a year had just handed me my dream job over lunch and was being so casual about it. Like it was no big deal. Bob and I had worked together off and on for months but had never spent more than two hours together. Yet here he was offering me the perfect position—in communications, for a Black-owned company, and I wouldn't have to leave DC. Thankfully I knew enough about job negotiations to hide my excitement.

"That's an interesting offer, Bob," I said. "I'll definitely give it some thought."

I floated back to Steptoe and Johnson, counting down the days until I handed in my notice. But when I mentioned the opportunity to Ty, he was much less enthusiastic.

"Terrible idea. You don't want to go over there now. Bob's having all these problems. There is no legal department to speak of. It'd be such a headache." I was crestfallen. Ty was one of the only partners who truly took an interest in me and seemed to want me to succeed as a lawyer. If he thought BET was a bad idea, then perhaps it was.

Months went by, and I never heard back from Bob about the general counsel position. More time passed before I began to worry that despite being my mentor, Ty may have other issues on his mind. BET was his client; if I went to the company as GC, then Ty would lose some of the the business he brought into the firm as a partner. Was he thinking of himself and his own business? I was concerned that I was being held in limbo to serve someone else's agenda. I had to take care of the situation myself. I picked up the phone.

"Good afternoon, Debra. Do you want me to put Bob on the line?" asked his assistant.

"No, no, no. I want to come in and see him," I told her. This wasn't a phone conversation. It'd been six months since Bob had offered me the job, and we'd never spoken about it again. I needed a face-to-face.

"I was wondering where you stood," said Bob when I sat down in front of his desk and asked if the job he'd offered me in the fall was still mine for the taking. He acted as if whole seasons hadn't passed since we'd last spoken about the general counsel role. "This is great timing! And there's an empty office downstairs with a wall of shelves for all your legal books. It's perfect. Let's do it."

And that was that. We shook hands, and at 32, I became BET's first general counsel, charged with creating and leading the legal department of what was then essentially a start-up.

Steptoe was paying me $68,000 a year at the time. Bob offered me $50,000.

"I don't think I can accept that," I told him during our compensation negotiation, one of many we'd have over the years. "This position would be great, but that pay cut is much too steep."

"I'm sorry, but I pay everyone the same," said Bob, who always maintained that all his senior executives made the same base salary and received the same bonuses year over year. He called the approach egalitarian.

I didn't know what to say. This job was too good to pass up, but an $18,000 pay cut? I'd worked my way to that $68,000 at Steptoe, and I was proud of that paycheck. It wasn't about the money so much as the recognition. Would taking less mean I didn't know my worth and my value to a company like BET, which sorely needed legal help? I wanted this job, but I didn't want to do more work for less. I'm certain Bob could see the wheels turning in my head because he suddenly clapped his hands together as if he'd just had an epiphany. "I have a solution!" he said. I hoped it was more money.

"We have casual Fridays here! Think of all the money you'll save on clothes, Debra."

Was he serious? The look on Bob's face said "yes." Although I knew full well that casual Fridays would never make up for a 26 percent pay cut, I accepted.

I didn't have footsteps to follow. There were no women, aside from my mother, who were examples to me on how to lead, manage, and climb the ladder. Professor Ferguson, Judge Parker, and Ty Brown were all mentors, helping me make decisions—good and bad—that propelled me forward. I wasn't Debra—the whipsmart legal mind who didn't need to command a courtroom to be powerful and who deserved to forge her own unique way forward. No, I was another cog in their own machines. A success story waiting to happen if only I listened to them and followed their rules. The judge and my law school professor were both mentors once I'd passed their tests. But that punishing process nearly broke me. I could have easily stayed in pieces on the floor with no one there to pick them up and put them back together.

Bob was different. He would become both my mentor *and* my sponsor. From the beginning, he wanted to see me succeed. He kept stretching me. He'd give me assignments outside the legal department. He believed in the quality of my work and that I could do anything that he asked me to do. That became apparent on my very first day at BET.

I'd been in my new office all of 10 minutes before I heard a knock on my door. Every office was glass except for Bob's. There were only a few of us in the building, and at any given moment, you could glance up, look across the floor, and see exactly what your colleague was doing. "Come in," I said, and in waltzes Bob in a pinstriped Armani suit with a few sheets of paper in his hand.

"Tell me what you think," he said, passing the contract to me to look over as he stood there assessing me. It was the settlement agreement between BET and the producer who'd handed in the subpar show. I was taken aback by Bob's immediate confidence in me. In all my years at Steptoe working on major clients, it was still rare to have anyone flat-out ask me what I thought about anything. But I wasn't that young lawyer anymore. As general counsel of an emerging media company, I had to get used to the added responsibility—and fast. Bob was waiting for my answer.

CHAPTER FIVE

UNAPOLOGETICALLY BLACK

Working at BET in the early days felt like a movie—actually, one film in particular: *Boomerang*. Rumor had it that the 1992 romantic comedy about an impossibly suave advertising executive (played by Eddie Murphy) on his way to conquering the corporate world—and half the women of Harlem—was based on Bob and BET. But I'm not talking about all the steamy office affairs (although there were always whispers floating around about those). Our DC headquarters itself was a scene with so much Black excellence on display from one frame to the next. One of the things Bob did brilliantly was curate an unapologetic environment of Black professionals. This was the 1980s, and there weren't many examples of young, successful, and sleek businesses run by and for Black people. Bob set a trend. He wanted a world-class company that walked the walk and talked the talk.

Here's the quick story of how the company was founded. As a former high-level Hill staffer, by 1979 Bob was working as a lobbyist for the National Cable & Telecommunications Association. His job was to take cable company CEOs and programmers up to Capitol Hill to meet with lawmakers, leveraging policy and business relationships to help deregulate the field. It was a very Washington job that a man like Bob was made for. At around five-foot-six with a tennis player's build, no one would call Bob intimidating, but his pull was undeniable. He was charismatic, funny, and smart—the class clown and class president rolled into one. More than that, Bob had an expert knowledge of the budding programming business that he could synthesize for anyone. I'd witnessed that myself when I first met Bob at BET's Georgetown office and he'd broken down the "must carry" laws for me while I was an associate at Steptoe. On that first visit, I was bowled over by everything—the classy office, the impeccably dressed staff, the sophisticated environment.

"Paint it Black" was a go-to Bobism. In fact, it was the founding principle of the company. One of his clients at the NCTA had come up with the idea for cable programming targeted toward the elderly. On their way to meet with congressmembers about the potential network, Bob asked if he could take a look at the proposal. There was a ton of data about the elderly demographic's potential viewership, buying power, and overall consumer habits. After glossing over the proposal, a light bulb went off in Bob's head: "Well, this would work for Black people." He asked if he could borrow the template, and Bob crossed out elderly and wrote in Black. That was the start of Black Entertainment Television. He was 33 at the time.

Telecom industry heavyweight John Malone was an early investor, loaning Bob $500,000 to get Black Entertainment

Television from page to programming. "Keep your revenues up and your costs down," John advised. That was one of our cornerstones at the company. Make money, don't spend it. It meant that all the executives were paid the same regardless of their workload. It's also why we did a lot of low-cost programming in the beginning, cementing our initial dependence on music videos and the music industry. Bob was never enamored by Hollywood or the prestige cable programmers like HBO and Showtime who were trying to compete with network television. But that didn't mean he didn't want us to look the part.

People strutted through the glass doors of the corporate office at 9 a.m. on the dot dressed to the nines. The colors were bold—burgundy, bright yellow, electric blue—and our collective confidence even more so. Bob revved up 31st Street each morning in his black Jaguar, shooting in like a bullet. His suits were custom Italian. His initials "RLJ" were engraved on the cuffs of his starched white shirts. All that swagger hung in the air, pumping into our office like oxygen. The rest of us took his lead. We all felt it. Remember when Bob claimed that casual Fridays would help me save a few dollars? Not even close. That office was a fashion show and woe the executive who didn't clock in looking like anything other than an *Ebony* magazine cover star. It was a sexy place to be. The atmosphere was electric from the first day I walked through those doors to join the team. Well, almost. Because when Bob first introduced me, the eye rolls were loud.

Only about 20 people worked in the corporate headquarters at the Hamilton Court location off M Street, a converted townhouse with a giant tree growing through it. The rest of the company working in programming and production was based out of a studio we rented in Virginia. The Georgetown clique was close-knit; a majority of the senior team had been there since the company's birth five years before, taking a chance on Bob's vision. I was the new girl, and if I was nervous about fitting in, Bob certainly didn't make it any easier.

"Everyone, this is Debra Lee," announced Bob at our weekly executive meeting. "She's our new general counsel, and you can no longer move forward with agreements or deals on your own. Don't sign anything without the legal department's approval." I *was* the legal department. Bob effectively told everyone at the table—a group of five other accomplished executives who'd been in the trenches with Bob, building up the company from just an idea to something tangible—that I was now looking over their shoulders. Folks shifted in their seats a bit, giving me the obvious once-over. By the time Bob sat down to get on with the rest of the business for the day, my cheeks were on fire. He had just introduced me as the wet blanket, placing the newbie between him and the rest of the team. (This rock and a hard place would come up again later.) I could tell by the curt nods and sideways glances that no one was thrilled about it. *Well, that went well,* I thought after the meeting as I headed back to my empty office. Oh, and about that office.

When Bob offered me the job, one of the perks he mentioned, aside from casual Fridays, was the first-class office I would get as general counsel. "It was practically built for you," he said, ever the salesman. "It's lined with bookshelves, perfect for all your law books." I could picture that big, important office in my head—books on books on books, my diplomas from Brown and Harvard framed on the wall, a giant leather chair from which to think my deep legal thoughts. Bob was right—it would be perfect.

I daydreamed about mahogany shelves filled from end to end with thick leather-bound tomes on my way into work that first

Monday morning. This was really happening. I was the 32-year-old general counsel of an entire media company. The enormity of all that responsibility didn't really hit me until our office manager, May, walked me to my new command center. "And this is you," she said, doing Vanna White hands in front of my first-floor space. I opened the door and felt the true weight of what I'd gotten myself into. The room *was* perfect. There was an entire wall with bookshelves from one end to the other just like Bob said. And they were completely empty. Not one book or even a speck of dust to spare between them. I had a choice here. I could either see it as simply bare, which it was, or as a blank canvas. One image could easily weigh me down, while the other would inspire. I realized then for the first time since accepting the job that the buck stopped at the door that read "Debra Lee, General Counsel." I'd been so excited to leave behind the unfulfilling work at Steptoe that I nearly forgot that stepping into more purposeful work would require starting from scratch. The firm had an expansive law library. Here I was, the one in charge, with not a book in sight. I had to get to work, and as I would soon find out, things at BET moved fast.

After Bob's announcement that morning, it took a while for the rest of the team to come around to the fact that he'd really meant it—they had to go through me if they wanted their programming to make it on air. Little by little the knocks at my door started coming, which opened the floodgates. But the first knock on that first day, of course, came from the man himself.

"Debra, I need you to look over this settlement agreement," he said, handing me a thick stack of papers from a production company that had sued BET for breach of contract. This was the legal headache that prompted Bob to offer me the role of GC in the first place. That contract was one of the reasons Bob knew he needed his own legal department. "Please review it and let me know what you think." That one sentence stopped me in my tracks. In all my years as a working lawyer, no one had asked for *my* legal opinion. I know that sounds completely bonkers, but it's true. The life of a young associate isn't about opinions, it's about document review, reading, researching. Clerking for Judge Parker and working at Steptoe, no one cared about what I thought. No one asked my opinion. I was there to write memo after memo after memo. Opinions? Keep those to yourself. But my name was on the door and those days were long gone. What I thought mattered now. I mattered. I was the expert. It took a second to find my voice in that moment, as shocked as I was.

"Ah, yeah, sure, Bob. I'll get this back to you with my thoughts," I managed to say, taking the agreement from Bob and hugging it to my chest like it was precious. This company was relying on me to protect it. It was one of the first times in my career that I felt true ownership over the work I was doing, a deep responsibility.

I must have read that agreement 20 times over the next week. I was educated and experienced, but trusting my own opinion still felt foreign. Truly inhabiting a new role with more responsibility isn't simply marked by a change in title or paycheck, it's a mindset. I had to tap into the self-confidence that had been building in me since I'd found the courage to leave Big Law in the first place. I'd trained for this; I'd worked alongside some of the smartest legal minds in the field. More importantly, I *was* a brilliant legal mind. Bob saw it, and so should I. After my week was up (you never wanted to keep Bob waiting), I climbed the glass staircase wrapped around the tree to Bob's office on the third floor and handed him back the settlement. "You can sign this. It's fine."

Eventually more work started flying my way.

"Almost, Jeff," I called from behind the door. He could see me in there.

"Debi, come on! Donnie goes out in three hours. Just give it the green light and let me get to the control room," demanded Jeff Lee, who was in charge of programming and production. Jeff was a big burly teddy bear of a guy, and despite the fact that he was huffing and puffing at my door, Jeff was one of my favorites. I considered him an ally on a small senior team of six executives, which included the two of us; James Ebron, who headed ad sales; Janice Thomas, who was head of advertising services; Curtis Symonds, who handled affiliate sales; and Antonia Duncan, the company's chief financial officer. Jeff was absolutely hysterical and would have an entire conference room in stitches in seconds. Because he needed me to get his programming on the air on time, we became fast friends.

"Just put your John Hancock on it! It's so easy," said Jeff as he marched into my office and loomed over my desk with a pen in hand. "Here, I'll help. D-E-B..."

"No way," I replied without looking up, with my red pen in one hand and a palmful of M&Ms in the other. "I'll be done soon."

Our work bringing programming to previously ignored Black audiences was meaningful and thrilling. We were doing something no one else was. So there were no guardrails—everything was on the table. Another favorite Bobism was "have fun and make money."

Bob was building this fast-paced company, and part of my job as general counsel was to make sure it was done right, or as close to right as possible so that we wouldn't get into any legal trouble. Because BET's legal department began and ended with me, I spent my first months in the law library downtown trying to build an archive of model contracts the programming department could follow moving forward so that executives would have legal references for future deals. Anything that aired on the channel had to go through me. Which is why Jeff was taking up space in my office demanding that I finish dotting the i's on a deal because *Video Soul*, our marquee music video program hosted by Donnie Simpson, was taping that night and Donnie wanted a surprise guest to stop by. But, of course, instead of clearing the appearance contract with legal (again me) ahead of time, Jeff waited until the 11th hour. That was life at BET. We were doing everything, and it all had to get done now.

Before I came on as general counsel, there was no one, besides Bob, telling anybody no. Then one day this young lawyer came along sucking a little bit of the fun out of it with her red pen and endless questions. But I took my job seriously. "One good lawsuit—just one—and BET is finished," I'd warn Bob whenever the pair of us would get into a legal discussion. (The man swore up and down he was a lawyer.) Eventually folks got it and started to send me draft agreements to review. Slowly but surely, the papers on my desk started piling up.

The work was breakneck, but none of us minded because we all were sprinting to the same finish line—"Have fun and make money"—barreling in the same direction, doing something that had never been done and needed to be done. Being at BET back then was like being an entrepreneur. We were writing the rules as we went. And once the company went public (more on that later), we had the capital to experiment and expand the brand in other businesses: credit cards, restaurants, casinos, clothing lines, magazines. I felt comfortable there, as if I could be my whole self and not a watered-down version of me, one that was safe and palpable. It was as if I was more alive—the colors were brighter, the fashions more fashionable, the conversations more urgent.

Working at the firm was hard, but BET was something else. You weren't billing hours, but you *were* trying to impress Bob, who was never satisfied with your last win. "What's next?" was his favorite question. Running a legal department of one meant that I always had an answer. On any given day I'd be working on Donnie Simpson's talent contract, trying to fix a problem with a broadcast deal in order to get a new program on the air in the next hour, or reviewing real estate deals for our new television studio in Northeast DC. The work was endless, but, oh, it was exciting. So, despite the fact that I was chained to my desk those first few years I also felt free. We were moving fast, but we could always go faster.

—

"Do you think we can go any faster?" I asked, checking my watch for the third time: 5:17 p.m. and rush hour. We had exactly 13 minutes to get all the way from the commercial printer's office in Virginia to the U.S. Securities and Exchange Commission on Capitol Hill. Bob's voice was playing on repeat in my head like the countdown for a bomb: *Get it done in five, four, three, two…*

"I'll try, Ms. Lee," assured Tony, my driver. I checked my wrist again, mentally willing every red light to turn green as we sped down Pennsylvania Avenue toward BET's future. Sitting in my lap was the most important stack of papers I'd ever produced—BET's Securities & Exchange registration, the first step in taking the company public on the New York Stock Exchange. We'd be the first Black-owned and -operated company to do it—ever. And we were late.

"The office closes at 5:30." Could he hear the worry in my voice?

"I'll get you there."

With my fingers, ankles, and toes crossed, I whispered a quiet prayer in the back seat before flipping through BET's filing for the hundredth and hopefully last time.

For five years, I had watched BET grow from the little media company that could to a formidable player in the budding cable industry. It was 1991, and cable networks were now reaching millions of households, a ripe gold mine to potential advertisers. But to take our business to the next level, BET needed capital, and that meant going public, selling off a portion of the company to shareholders, and using the money raised to invest in expanding the brand. This was a major deal. We were a Black company, and Wall Street had come calling. As general counsel, the IPO filing fell squarely on my shoulders. For the past 10 months, I had lived and breathed the process, poring over every aspect of our application to make sure it was airtight. All-nighters were a given. By then I had a husband and a toddler at home, but this took precedence. I spearheaded everything regarding our registration with the SEC, which involved meticulously detailed statements about BET's real estate holdings, business practices, management structure, and financials. It was a massive undertaking that Bob, of course, wanted yesterday. The work was grueling, but because I believed so strongly in our mission, it never seemed like a slog.

The filing was akin to a biography about BET. It was hundreds and hundreds of pages describing every aspect of the business. We had to lay out the company's origin story, how it was structured internally, what our business model and growth looked like, what the risks of going public were, and so much more. It was a bird's-eye view of BET's corporate health. Compiling that complicated story for the IPO meant that at around 6 p.m. each day, after running the legal department, I would dash over the Potomac River to Virginia to spend the next five hours crafting our filing with our outside legal counsel from Skadden Arps. The printers set up a room for us in the back, and the two of us attorneys would proof the previous day's pages, catching typos, fixing language, editing, editing, and editing. It had to be perfect. We got lost in the maze of it every night, looking up at around 10 p.m. and realizing neither one of us had eaten anything.

"Chinese?"

"Is that place down the street still open?"

The answer was invariably no, and I'd head to the front desk of the printer for another handful of M&Ms, which I assume they kept on hand just for us.

Weeks and months were flying by while the IPO filled my working hours and my dreams. Fine, I was a wee bit obsessed, particularly because I knew we had to be twice as good. Reams of paperwork filled every inch of my office. I double- and then triple-checked everything. Perfect was not an option, it was a must.

Finally, Bob reached the limit of his patience. "We're filing this thing on Wednesday, Debi. Done or not."

So there I was in the back of a speeding black car reading one of the most important documents I'd written in my entire professional career. I took one last look at our application just to make sure everything was in order, and that's when I spotted it— a typo! And then another one and another one. I looked at my watch again. We had less than 10 minutes to make it to the SEC building. There was no way I could turn around, run back to my desk, correct the mistakes on my computer, head to the printer, and then head back to the SEC before it closed. But this filing had to be perfect. I had to be perfect. I fished a black pen from my purse and started crossing out words and writing corrections in the margins.

I was used to course-correcting like this. I'd been doing it since I was a baby. Because of Dad's military career, before my tenth birthday, our family of five (Mom, Dad, my older sister Gretta, my older brother Ron, and me) would live in South Carolina, Germany, Washington, DC, and Compton, California. Change had become second nature to me. Trading one country for the next, one city for another. Adding another elementary school to my résumé, a new set of friends to replace the ones I left behind. I never got too comfortable in one place because I knew how quickly the rug could be pulled from underneath my feet. Nothing was so deeply rooted it couldn't be snatched up and replanted. The near constant shifts happening in my life were always made easier because of my unwavering commitment to hard work. Because if there was also a constant in my life, it was success.

I was always powerfully smart. It was my anchor. Drop me in an unfamiliar environment with new faces and new benchmarks and I might be quiet, but I was always absorbing and achieving. Doing well steadied and soothed me. I had the satisfaction of knowing that my status as the forever new kid never meant I wasn't the smartest in the room. I got good at crossing out one line and rewriting my story. In fact, that's what led me to the back seat of that car in the first place. From the shy student to the Ivy League grad to the Big Law associate and now senior executive of what was poised to be the next great American success story; none of those steps in my climb were preordained. Every move was improvised. I mean, here I was, the can-do general counsel of *the* Black company of the moment, and 20 years ago I hadn't even wanted to go to law school.

"You're much too pretty to be a lawyer," Muhammad Ali

whispered in my ear one afternoon. He'd shown up to meet with Bob about a potential project, and Bob being Bob had walked the Champ down our spiral staircase so that everyone got the chance to see the legend. But they stopped at my office to say hi. We shook hands, and Ali leaned in to deliver the news that my looks didn't match my title. I didn't know whether to be shocked or flattered—but I settled on the latter. That's what being at BET was like back then. Never, ever dull. The work would surprise you, steady you, and make you smile. I wanted more of that out in the world and the IPO would get us there. As long as I could catch every typo while in the backseat and make it to the agency on time.

—

With less than five minutes to go, I shot out of the back of the car clutching BET's SEC filing to my chest. I was practically hyperventilating. The first Black company to IPO on the NYSE was turning in an application with my pen marks. I couldn't believe it. But Bob wanted this thing in by Wednesday, and that was that. When I ran into the building's lobby, still anxious, my mood changed on a dime.

At the end of the light-speckled lobby inside the SEC building, there was a counter with three Black people behind it. When they saw me running through the glass doors, my heels clicking loudly against the marble floors, everyone looked up from their work. All eyes were on me. Even with just minutes left to get the filing in that day, I took a moment to take in the room. This was the Securities and Exchange Commission, the government agency I had dreamed of working for when I'd graduated from Harvard so many years before. But here I was on the other side of the counter. Instead of doing policy work, I was a powerful lawyer and corporate executive. The journey hadn't so much come full circle but down a zigzagging path that somehow had reached the same destination. I looked in the delighted faces of the people behind that counter and realized in that split second that I was exactly where I was supposed to be.

"You're going where? To work for whom?" None of my colleagues at Steptoe could get their minds around me leaving when I resigned. Why would I give up a well-paid position at a prestigious law firm to join, what? A cable programming company? For Black people? We didn't even *have* cable in 1986 DC. No one had seen BET on their television, much less heard of the fledgling network. Joining a start-up wasn't just outside the well-trodden Washington career track, it was plain nuts. But my presence at the SEC that afternoon had proved all those negative voices wrong.

"Hi, I'm Debra Lee, and I'm filing the registration paperwork for BET Holdings' initial public offering," I told the Black woman smiling at me behind the counter. I checked my watch for the final time. 5:28, *tick, tick, tick.* The receptionist gave me a look that I can't forget. Her face went from shock to elation in seconds. "Congratulations," she said loud enough for her colleagues— mostly Black folks—to hear. Everyone turned to look. "She's from BET," the woman said, pointing at me and my precious stack of papers. "They're planning to IPO." The staff clapped and cheered as I handed over the application just under the wire. They were beaming at me. They were so excited. It was 1991 and the first time they'd seen a Black company file paperwork for an IPO on the New York Stock Exchange. This moment wasn't just mine, it belonged to them, too.

I glanced down at the final documents I'd spent months preparing: "This is a moment," I told myself. It was a true celebration—the Black SEC staffers high-fived me as I delivered the final paperwork. It made all the late nights at the printers and the M&Ms worth it.

That was what working for "the man" could look like. Corporate America could be filled with pride and purpose. It could be giant smiles on the faces of total strangers, who, of course, weren't strangers at all. We were all in this fight together to see ourselves and succeed in spaces not built for us. It was a watershed moment for them. Just a slight opening to the wider door of what BET could be. And who I could be working for a place like that. For me, that realization was a turning point.

Growing up in the South as the child of both the civil rights movement and the Black Power movement, working for "the man" was akin to selling your soul to the devil. I was raised on a steady diet of Black love, social justice, and community responsibility. Back then, being beholden to profit margins was considered antithetical to "the cause." I wanted to impact my community and save the world. Joining Big Law or Corporate America was like joining the dark side—and I'd done both.

But BET, on the verge of transforming from a start-up to a major American business success story, was more than just another corporation. We meant something, and all the jobs I'd had before had led me there. Not every company is creating cultural change, not every position you'll have will feel like both a personal and professional evolution. But that doesn't mean you're wasting your time. It means you're building, you're watering, you're preparing for that big moment when it all comes together. I was pulling late nights at the printers to make it to the SEC that afternoon. Next, Bob and the other corporate executives set out on "the sexy road show," traveling the country on a private jet trying to gin up excitement with investment firms and big ticket investors for the initial public offering.

The night before the company was to go public with a splashy celebration at the New York Stock Exchange on Wall Street, Bob and the senior executive team all flew to Manhattan for opening day. The plane was vibrating with excitement about what the next morning would be like. "Hey, how much do you think the stock will skyrocket?" and "How rich do you think Bob is going to be after this?" bounced around the seats as everyone had fun predicting how bright our futures would be come morning. It felt like a bus ride to a big homecoming game—the football squad hyping itself up on the W within reach. But I couldn't join in. I sat quietly in my window seat peering out at the dark clouds and mentally going over the legal details of our IPO. All I could think about was everything that could still go left. What if our valuation was wrong? What if the stock plummeted in the first five minutes? What if? This was my biggest career achievement to date, and my neck was still on the line.

About a week before, I had gotten a call from Harold Doley, the first Black person to purchase a seat on the exchange in 1973.

"I hear you all are getting ready to start trading next week," said Harold. The pride in his voice reached through the phone. This milestone was his—and that of every Black man and woman who'd been shut out of Wall Street—as much as it was ours.

"It would be an honor for me to stand with you all on the floor. Is that possible?" he asked. When the BET group arrived at the NYSE the next morning, Harold Doley was waiting for us.

Initial public offerings are like Christmas morning. Everyone is excited. The possibilities seem limitless in those weighty minutes before the starting bell of the day rings. We arrived en masse to the NYSE's historic building on the corner of Wall Street and Broad in Manhattan's financial district just past dawn. The market opens at 9:30 a.m. on the dot, and there is a lot of pomp and circumstance for the company beforehand. First, we attended a pre-opening breakfast in the ballroom above the trading floor, where we received commemorative medals marking the event and a peek at the ceremonial gavel. It was a whirlwind, and at each step, our small team of Black executives could feel the positive energy in the room, especially from the dozens of Black people who worked there. We got head nods, handshakes, and more than a few high fives. This was big business—the Corporate America I had been so against as a young woman—and it wasn't at all bad.

If upstairs is all pomp and circumstance, then downstairs, on the actual floor of the stock exchange, is straight chaos. Walking on the trading floor is a shock to the system. The place is massive, like a small country all on its own. And the noise? Buyers are screaming their stock orders at the top of their lungs, and sellers are yelling right back. Tickets are flying. Floor brokers in their signature blue jackets are sprinting past one another across the cavernous marketplace trying to get deals done. And it's barely past 9:30 in the morning. I was surprised by how insane it all seemed. Upstairs in the gilded boardroom, the mood was celebratory and civilized. But the floor was pandemonium.

"How do people work here every day?" I shouted over to Bob, who was doing something like a power stance near the entrance we had just walked through. He was grinning from ear to ear, soaking in all the racket, bright lights, and confetti.

"Isn't it incredible?" he said before heading over to join us in the VIP area they had set up for the staff that had traveled up from Washington.

Everyone at the NYSE is superstitious. If the ceremonial opening bell doesn't ring for exactly 10 seconds, the traders on the floor will boo the executive—loudly. Bob had been contemplating that timing for weeks. But he never got the chance. That morn-ing Bob Johnson, who in 15 years had successfully brought a Black-owned business to the oldest and largest stock exchange in the country, did not ring the ceremonial bell. I don't know what the reasoning behind that decision was. We took it in stride, of course. This was still our day. But none of us could help but won-der if things would have played out differently for a white com-pany. I say we wondered, but we all knew the answer.

Despite that hiccup, BET had an outstanding opening. We knocked it out of the park. Trading started at $17 and quickly shot up to $25. When the market closed at 4:30 p.m. that day, our stock was worth $23.50. Bob became an instant millionaire. His initial investors made millions. And as far at the business went, BET Holdings, our parent company, raised upward of $70 million to reinvest in our future. Our mouths hung open the entire day. The impact was enormous. It wasn't until the final bell rang (that one goes for 15 seconds) that it really hit me. It wasn't just the last 10 months of obsessively working on the IPO that had come to fruition. It was my entire career path up to that point. When I'd joined BET five years before, the company had just turned prof-itable. Now we were big business. The shift was dizzying, but it confirmed that I'd made the right choice jumping from the firm to a small cable programming company no one had ever heard of. That day at the stock exchange, we felt like a true corporation.

"You made this happen, Debra," said Bob as the day ended and the group of us headed out to celebrate. Bob and his wife, Sheila, went to a fancy restaurant uptown to toast the day, while the executive vice presidents hopped in cabs going north on the West Side Highway to have our own celebratory lunch at Rob-ert DeNiro's restaurant, the Tribeca Grill. Bob hadn't given any of us stock in the company before the IPO—a regular practice for start-ups today—so while the company's bigwigs had become super rich in minutes, the rest of us were...not. It was a sobering reality that, to be completely honest, dampened our joy a tad. But it was still our moment.

I'd helped usher in this success behind the scenes, and now BET was standing in front of the world: a publicly traded company. We were an American success story, not just a Black success story.

On the flight back to DC, the muscles in my body started to relax for the first time in months. I no longer had doomsday scenarios running through my mind at all hours. We'd done it. I'd done it. It was over. I could finally spend more than 10 minutes with my kids before rushing off to work, maybe even go out to dinner with my husband, Randy, or take a real vacation.

The next day at work it was back to business as usual. Not five minutes after I'd had my morning coffee, Bob walked into my office with a question: "When do you expect all the legal paperwork for the transponder purchase to be done?" I looked at him like he had two heads. Really? Already? That's when I created my personal slogan for life at BET: "absolutely no downtime." With Bob, there was always another deal waiting in the wings. Sure, we'd pop champagne and pat ourselves on the back for a job well done. But downtime? Not when there was a stack of new contracts to sign and more money to be made. He was on to his next one, before the ink dried on the last idea.

The pace could easily wear you down—*how could it not?*—but because everyone at BET believed wholeheartedly that they were building a legacy brick by brick and side by side, the arduous work seemed worth the back pain. And for the most part that was true. There was just one problem: I had a legacy of my own to build at home as a new mom. People often refer to the juggle of work–life balance, and it tickles me. Juggling sounds easy. What I was doing as a wife, new mother, lawyer, and executive was more like a struggle. And the work wouldn't wait for you to figure it all out. My solution was always trying to do the impossible, until I couldn't.

CHAPTER SIX

WHAT BALANCE?

"Let me ask you a question," said Bob, taking his eyes off the road for a split second to face me.

"Sure," I replied, shifting in the passenger's seat of Bob's Jag for the umpteenth time. I was heavily pregnant with my first child, Quinn, and had been trying to find a semi-comfortable position. We were on our way to a permits meeting for BET's new production studio in Northeast DC. I'd added the $10 million construction to my list of responsibilities, overseeing the process from blueprints to keys. No matter how big I got, I showed up to the building site to survey our progress with a hard hat on my head and size eight men's shoes on my swollen feet.

"Okay shoot," I said after finally achieving a tiny modicum of comfort in those buttery leather seats.

"What do you and Randy have planned for when it's time?" asked Bob in all seriousness. I almost laughed. Was he for real? Knowing Bob, absolutely. See, there had been no official or even unofficial maternity leave policy at BET when I'd joined five years before. They'd never needed one. I was the first senior executive at the company to get pregnant. So as general counsel and head of the legal department, I wrote the policy from scratch as my own belly grew bigger.

The corporate standard at the time was six weeks off with your job waiting when you got back. I wanted a full three months, which was completely unheard of, especially among senior executives. This was 1989; women were still relative unicorns in the corporate world…and pregnant women? Even more rare. But I knew—at least I thought I knew—what new mothers needed, and that was time. Time to rest, time to bond, and time away from work. I did my research, asking the top executives I knew what their own companies were doing, and used that information to put a new maternity leave policy together as part of the employee handbook I was already rewriting, and Bob approved it. On my calendar for May 8 was one word: "baby."

"Randy's going to drive me to the hospital. I have a bag packed ready to go," I told Bob. Talking about my growing belly and what was going to happen on the other side was not our regular office banter. Where was he going with this?

"Well, if you're at work when it happens, just let Randy know I would be happy to drive you to the hospital and meet him there," said Bob.

"Uh, thank you," I replied, still squirming in my seat. But in my head, I was thinking, *The last thing I want is for my water to break in Bob Johnson's precious Jaguar.*

"No problem," said Bob, smiling as we pulled into our massive construction zone near W Street Northeast in a depressed section of Washington that no one wanted to spend money on. BET was breaking ground in more ways than one as a Black-owned company unafraid to invest in the real DC. I hoisted myself out of the passenger side, grabbed my white hard hat, and wobbled over to my site manager for our daily progress report.

That was my introduction to what life would be like as a working mom—the baby wouldn't stop the work, and the work didn't slow down for the baby. The two were always intertwined. There wasn't one without the other. Women are often told that their careers will inevitably suffer the moment they become mothers. Men, of course, never get this damaging message. They're allowed their ambition as fathers and husbands. This was the same subtle message I heard loud and clear at the firm when Steptoe gently steered female attorneys on "the family track," which meant wills and estates legal work instead of more rigorous litigation. The assumption is that motherhood and career ambition simply don't mix. Don't believe that—ever. It's a lie.

Growing my family didn't dampen my ambition at work one bit. If anything, it added fuel. In fact, my first years of motherhood coincided with some of my biggest career leaps. What was true, however, is that my success as a mother and businesswoman required more of everything—more help at home, more time in the office, and more grace. Because in 1990, gender roles and expectations had not changed enough to lift the lion's share of parenting responsibilities from my shoulders. Heck, decades later, the job is still unfairly lopsided. As mothers we do more—period. I say fight against that, change policies, speak up, be honest, and don't try to work as if you don't have kids. But I also want to advise you to prepare for just how hard it will be to do both. That's something I wish I'd known.

Throughout my pregnancy with Quinn, I never knew which would come first—the new studio building or the baby. Pushing it to the last possible moment, I waddled to the ribbon cutting exactly 39 weeks and 6 days pregnant.

"Don't you think you should stay home, Debi?" asked my husband Randy.

"You know I can't miss it. I've been working on this project for over a year. Marion Barry is going to be there. Bob's got this fancy party planned afterward. It's going to be a whole to-do. We *have* to go."

"Okay, okay, you're right," said Randy, the voice of reason while also conceding to his very pregnant and very hormonal wife. "Let's just not stay too late."

My second husband, Randy, and I met at a Communications Bar Luncheon four years after my divorce from Ernie. Randy, who was working for American Satellite Corporation, knew a close guy friend of mine. He was smart, great-looking, and quiet. We used to spot each other on the bus cutting through Adams Morgan in the morning and wave. So when I saw Randy at the networking luncheon, I said hello by way of a peck on the cheek because I felt like I knew him (and did I mention he was handsome?). Before the event was over, he asked me out, and I just about fell over. We made plans right then and there to meet the next night at 8 p.m. on the corner of 18th Street and Columbia Road in the heart of Adams Morgan. Randy took me to his favorite watering holes in the neighborhood. Even though he was a highly successful communications attorney like me, he had passions outside of the law. Really he'd always wanted to be a filmmaker. He was debonair and cool, interested in fine art and good wine—so different from the normal stuffy Washington lawyer. We had a wonderful time on that first date, and all I wanted to do was spend more hours with him, but the next day I had to leave town for my grandmother's funeral. While I was at the wake, my sister Gretta asked me why I was smiling so darn much.

"I met this great guy," I told her, beaming way more than I should've been.

"And?"

"He's drop-dead gorgeous, but I don't remember if I gave him my number."

Turns out I did. When I got back to DC, Randy called. That was in October. We were engaged by May and married by August. It was a glorious 10-month romance. He swept me off my feet. I felt like we were on the same track—both lawyers, ambitious but fun-loving. We weren't in our 20s, still trying to figure out who we were as people. We were older—I was 30, and Randy was 31— with more confidence and clarity on what we wanted to be and whom we wanted to be that person with. Randy and I could create a beautiful life together, climbing and supporting each other. In reality, we weren't at all prepared for how difficult it would be to have two successful and driven people in a marriage. We'd assumed our roles would be fairly traditional—I would manage my career *and* the home while Randy rose up the ranks at his company. But titles change, paychecks grow, hours add up, and roles get flipped. We had never mapped out what to do when the road to our picture-perfect life together went through unexpected twists and turns. We didn't recalculate.

When I got the job at BET, Randy and I were still newlyweds. The week before my first day, Bob hosted an Oscar party in the Georgetown office's conference room. I took Randy, all too happy to show him off. At the beginning of the night, Bob passed out ballots so everyone could vote for who they thought would win. I, of course, had a secret weapon. Randy was a film buff, so between the two of us we managed to pick winners in practically every category, taking home the grand prize ourselves: a case of champagne. I remember thinking, *This is a good foot to start off on.*

Committed to our careers—him at American Satellite and me at BET, which expanded rapidly from 10 million subscribers when I first started to 22 million before our IPO—Randy and I decided to wait five years to have children. We knew we wanted to grow our family, but fitting that goal into our busy lives was a struggle. I went into the office the Sunday before my due date to wrap up a few projects, praying that the baby didn't have other ideas. At 5 o'clock the following morning, my water broke.

In truth, my maternity leave wasn't all that restful. Adjusting to life as a mom with a big, important job was made more difficult because I didn't have the support I needed at home or in the office. Randy didn't have paternity leave, and I naively assumed that life at home with a newborn would be easy. This was before everyone had a night nurse, a sleep trainer, and a nanny. I was on my own—and I'd actually planned it that way. I imagined waking up in the morning and seeing my husband off while the baby and I spent the day strolling through DC in matching outfits. That was not how it went. There were more than a few days when Randy would walk through the front door of our Adams Morgan condo at 6 p.m. and I'd still be in a bathrobe decorated with spit-up. My plan was to take three months off, adhering to the very policy I'd written myself. But what I failed to plan for—or, more accurately, what Bob failed to realize even after I explained it time and time again—was that the legal work wouldn't slow down just because I wanted it to. So not only did I not have the help at home all new mothers desperately need, but there was no one in the office to pick up that workload either. When I joined BET, Bob budgeted $100,000 for the company's legal department, which meant that after deducting my own salary, I had exactly $50,000 left for outside counsel, business travel, research books, and a summer intern.

I complained, but Bob acted confused. "Why would you need legal help? You're an attorney."

"I'm a communications attorney. That's my expertise. But there will be times when we need to get advice from other legal experts. I don't know *allll* the law."

"I think you can handle it," said Bob in that way he had. It was a mix of him having the utmost confidence in your ability to do whatever needed to be done—no matter the cost—and Bob's belief that if he willed it, it would happen. Yeah, I never got the budget increase. Instead, I prayed a whole lot, hoping against hope that we didn't get sued because of something I missed with all the contracts and legalese pouring through my hands. For a while, my workaround was having regular lunch dates with colleagues from other companies and law firms who didn't mind trading free advice for a free meal. But once I got pregnant—the enormity of my growing to-do list was as obvious as my growing belly—it was clear that something had to give.

A few months before Quinn was born, Bob made the unilateral decision that BET would now be charging our affiliates three cents to carry our programming, which meant we (I) had to rewrite every single contract we had with our carriers throughout the country. We're talking hundreds of deals that had to be renegotiated. I was the only lawyer in the building and growing more pregnant day by day. Bob and I had already gone head-to-head more times than I could count about increasing the legal budget, but this? This was beyond what even I could do. I knew it, and so did he.

"This is impossible," I told Bob after he announced the increase at an executive meeting. "There is no way I can get this done in time." But he'd committed to this new plan, which meant I was the one who had to see it through. For a week or two, I tried to make headway myself, but between these new deals, the new building, and the new baby coming, I needed to make the case once again for more support. In the beginning of my career, I would have been afraid or, worse, ashamed to ask for help. In the business world, we're conditioned to think that needing support is a sign of weakness because you can't hack it on your own. But that approach to work—to any part of your life—leads to burnout. And for what? Yes, I cared deeply about BET and would do anything to see it succeed. But at the risk of a nervous break- down? I think Bob must have seen the edge of the cliff in front of me because finally he reluctantly agreed to getting me legal help.

We hired a bright young lawyer named Lisa. She was eager but only a few years out of law school. So while having a junior attor- ney who could keep the legal gears moving was a huge weight lifted, she wasn't experienced enough to run the department on her own. I could relax, but only a little. Remember, one good law- suit and we'd be out of business. Work was never far from mind. Which is why I was still fielding calls and instructing Lisa on what to do from my delivery room at Washington Hospital Center.

"Debi? Really?" asked Randy, who returned to my bedside with a cup of ice chips only to find me on the phone with the office. Bob had made some more of his signature pronouncements at our regular Tuesday staff meeting, and Lisa was in a tizzy. I needed to talk her down and talk her through what had to be done.

I covered the bottom of the receiver with my hand and stage-whispered, "This is the last one. I promise." My husband shook his head, put the cup down, and proceeded to rub my back. Quinn arrived via cesarean later that day.

The rest of my leave didn't go any better. Randy would head out in the morning, and I'd make dreamy plans for Quinn and me to finally get to the park down the street, and then the phone would ring. "Debra, we need you." I was on conference calls while feeding Quinn, praying that he didn't cry, scandalizing the big-time lawyers on the other line by the fact that I was doing business with a baby on my breast. Being at home and trying to work while also trying to bond with my new baby was tearing me right down the middle.

Randy tried to help—but men can only do so much for a breast-feeding newborn. Plus, he had to go back to work after just two weeks. My mother, who'd moved to DC to be closer to me, planned to take care of Quinn during the day once I was back in the Georgetown office full time. But I had expressly told her that I could handle things until that time came. What was I thinking? I should have had my mother by my side from the moment I left the hospital, but I thought I was Superwoman. Randy's mom wanted to help too—and I was stubborn in my desire to do it all alone. "You all can come visit, but you're going to have to leave," I told them. Despite finding my voice and asking for help at work, what happened at home was another story. I was all caught up in the trap of expectations. Wasn't I built for this? Shouldn't I know how to take care of my son on my own? I was 35, an older mom by 1980s standards. I had three degrees and was a corporate lawyer. A week-old baby would be a piece of cake, right?

To say the very least, I vastly underestimated what a major adjustment life at home with a newborn would be. Everything fell on me. No matter how equal your relationship is before you have a child, once the baby arrives, the burden falls on the woman. It just does. Blame the patriarchy, public policy, all of it. But until there is a seismic cultural shift in this country, the responsibility is still there. In the meantime, I had a child to take care of and a career to keep afloat. Somehow, I managed to struggle through those first 12 weeks managing Quinn, conference calls, and even a work trip to New York. In the end, it was so nerve-racking trying to balance it all that I was relieved when it was finally time to go back to the office. (I wouldn't call it back to "work" because in truth I never stopped working.) At least then I could focus on one thing at a time. But if I thought my workload was a ton before the baby, things were only just getting started.

My first day back, Bob called a surprise senior staff meeting. None of us knew what he was planning to announce, but knowing our boss, it was going to be big—and it would mean more work for all of us. Jeff winked at me from across the conference room and mouthed "get ready" as Bob marched to the head of the table and clapped his hands together dramatically.

"I want to start a teen magazine, and I need somebody to run it," he announced, glancing around the room looking for any takers. A magazine? *Okaaaay.* Eyes went wide, but it wasn't exactly shocking. Bob always had his eureka moments. In fact, the idea made perfect sense when you thought about it. BET had yet to expand its brand outside of the cable industry, but the master plan was always to reach Black audiences wherever they were. And there were few general interest magazines speaking directly to the urban teen market with an uplifting and empowering tone. This all sounded pretty great, actually. I caught myself becoming slightly giddy at the thought of seeing something like this come together. I loved magazines. *Ebony* and *Jet* were like Bibles in our house growing up, and every year my mom took me to *Ebony*'s traveling Fashion Fair when it stopped in Greensboro. The ticket came with a year's subscription to the magazine, and I tore through them every month. I not-so-secretly always wanted to work at one. But just as that thought popped into my head, I swatted it down. *Debra, you just got back from maternity leave, a hard maternity leave. There is absolutely no way you're going to throw your hat in the ring. Now stop looking so darn excited.* I'd been back at work for a hot minute. There was a sweet little brown baby at home waiting for me to snuggle him in approximately seven hours, which reminded me that I needed to pump soon before my breasts started leaking milk through my silk blouse. Nope, I could never do that job in a million years. But I'd be happy to support whoever got it. As if he heard my thoughts, Jeff raised his hand.

"I'll do it," he said.

"No, not you," replied Bob all too quickly. Another hand went up. "No," said Bob. And then another and another until more than half the execs in the room had volunteered and all of them were shot down. I hadn't said a word. If anything, I was trying to shrink down in my seat, willing myself invisible until the moment passed. Eventually folks gave up, and Jeff asked, "Why don't you just tell us who you want to run it?"

Bob turned to his right—I always sat on Bob's right—and cocked an eyebrow. "Debra, I want you to do it."

Inside I groaned. Really? My breasts were engorged, and the bags under my eyes were barely concealed under makeup. Quinn had been up until 3 a.m. that very morning, and I was exhausted. The last thing I needed teetering on top of my overflowing plate was the title of magazine publisher. But on the other hand, running my own magazine was a dream. This was the type of creative and purpose-driven work I'd left the firm for. Building a magazine from the ground up that highlighted the lives of young Black teens—kids who reminded me of myself when I was protesting and marching as a student at Dudley High—was right in line with how I wanted to marry my work and my passion. I couldn't say no, and obviously, deep down, I didn't want to. Bob knew it too.

The room fell silent. I hadn't realized that everyone—including my boss—was waiting for my answer. So I did what all working mothers do—I figured it out.

"I'd be honored."

"Great," said Bob. "I want it on stands in a year." I didn't bat an eye.

First, I had to rent extra office space in Georgetown to house the magazine's editorial team. It had to be close to the Hamilton Court office in order for me to easily run from one meeting to the next during the day, switching hats from general counsel to magazine publisher as I dashed up Wisconsin Avenue. Then I had to hire folks to fill it and create what would become *YSB*, which stood for *Young Sisters and Brothers*. I named Frank Dexter Brown, an ambitious journalist who believed wholesale in our mission to uplift, our editor in chief. Next came Fo Wilson, an imaginative graphic artist from New York who got the visual sensibility of *YSB*—youthful, positive, and fun. She would be our art director. This was my first foray into building a team of my own. My goal was to hire professionals with vision and purpose. Frank and Fo both leapt at the opportunity to create something by and about Black folks. That was the power of the BET brand that we were just starting to realize then: Our audience and consumers were proud of the company, and they wanted to see us win.

But before we even had a concept for the premiere issue, Bob, of course, threw another curveball our way. He wanted the magazine to debut in May, which gave us less than six months instead of a year to pull the rest of the editorial staff together, assign articles, schedule photo shoots, pitch to advertisers, and complete the millions of other tasks that bring a magazine from concept to your mailbox.

"He can't be serious. Right?" asked Frank.

Oh, Frank. He was new and didn't know that when Bob fixed a target in his sights, there was no reasoning with him. The timeline was completely bonkers. We all knew that. It meant we wouldn't have time to print a test issue or roll out a 360-degree marketing strategy independent of the cable channel. But Bob wanted what he wanted.

"I'm afraid he is very serious," I told Frank. "Just tell me what you need, and I'll make sure you have it." What he didn't know was that I had already gone to the mat with Bob over the insane publishing schedule. Arguing with Bob over what was and wasn't possible was such a regular occurrence I should have jotted it down on my calendar:

9 a.m.: coffee
9:30 a.m.: attack the growing pile of contracts taking over my desk
11:30 a.m.: listen to Jeff complain I wasn't approving a new deal fast enough
12:30 p.m.: tell Bob there's was no way we could pull off XYZ task in time
12:45 p.m.: go back to my desk and figure out how to make the impossible possible

"It's only 68 pages with a couple of staples," Bob told me when I tried to get him to walk back the six-month deadline. "What does he mean 'impossible'? It's simple." I rolled my eyes. "It's simple" was another Bob proverb. It applied to anything and everything he could dream up. Nothing was too hard a task for the people Bob put his trust in—and that right there was the kicker. Even when he was asking for the moon, the man made you believe you could wrap it in a bow by close of business. He wasn't being an unreasonable tyrant—though he could take on that role when the mood hit him—but instead he simply had confidence in you. "It's simple."

We tore our hair out trying to make that deadline. And I was already running on fumes. Because while *YSB* was gearing up in 1991, I was also heading up the intense preparation for what would eventually become BET's incredibly successful initial public offering. But at the time all I knew was that I was staring down more work after almost every meeting. This is how my year was going: I gave birth to Quinn via C-section in May, got back to work by August, and was named publisher of a magazine, a dream job. A month after that, the IPO project was also on my plate. The following January I had an editorial leadership team in place for the magazine. We planned to print our first magazine that August, and opening day on the New York Stock Exchange would be in October.

I don't believe there is a word in the English dictionary to describe how overworked I was. Mentally I was always in three different places at once—with the baby, with the SEC, or with *YSB*. And physically I was all over the place. As a publishing neophyte I thought it would be smart to take a two-week publishing course at Stanford University in Palo Alto, California. Bob had confidence in me, but I wanted to have that same confidence in myself. I wanted to feel more prepared for the leadership role I was taking on.

That's a thing we do as women. We don't just dive in blindly; we prepare, prepare, prepare. Whether this more thoughtful approach is right or wrong I think depends on the outcome—and your timetable. Preparation can never be a bad thing. Who wouldn't want to know all there is to know about the industry they're in? I loved theorizing with my peers, studying consumer metrics, and absorbing information from proven experts. But you can't bury your head in the books for too long; the business is waiting. It's like my dad said after I kept signing up for African American studies classes at Brown—"Don't you know yourself by now?" If you spend all your time *thinking* and never *doing*, the preparation becomes a roadblock to your success instead of a speedway. Plus, the guys aren't doing all that. Trust me.

To make up for all the extra time I was spending outside the office, I kept a grueling schedule, never letting one job (wife, mother, attorney, publisher) dominate. That August I flew to California to spend a glorious week learning about the magazine business, then hopped on a plane back to Washington for a three-hour meeting with the bankers to get up to date on the IPO, and then flew down to Daytona Beach to watch the first issue of *YSB* come off the printing press. Then I flew back home to spend 24 hours with my husband and my baby before high-tailing it back to Stanford for the last week of the course. I thought I was invincible—and for a while I was. My mom stayed home with Quinn until he was a toddler; after that she threw in the towel. "Babies I can do, but all this crawling and carrying on? He's too much for me," she told me before heading back to work herself part-time. Randy was a successful lawyer in his own right, so something had to give. Daycare it was. If women want to be competitive in the corporate world, they have to have good, dependable, and affordable childcare. Let me say that again: There is no way, absolutely no way, I would have had the career that I had without quality and available childcare. Because 1991 was my year. I was crushing it at work. And waking up in cold sweats to prove it.

"No, no, no!" I jolted up from bed, my arm outstretched as if I had one last point to make.

"Debi, you're all right; Quinn is fine," said Randy, who was shaken from his sleep next to me and assumed I was worried about our one-year-old in the next room.

"Yes, yes, the baby," I said, rolling over to my side and gritting my teeth against the nightmare I'd just had where I was bounding up the spiral staircase that wrapped around the tree in the Georgetown office, holding Quinn like a football while taking the steps two at a time. At every floor there was another faceless employee shouting, "Debra, we need you!" Quinn was sleeping peacefully as I tried to make it to the safety and solitude of the penthouse floor, but the stairs wouldn't stop; they just kept going up and up and up.

The yo-yo of life as a working mom had me tied up in knots even in my sleep. I was exhilarated and exhausted. Living my dream and having nightmares. In under a year, I'd effectively made the leap from the legal side to the business side, which is extremely rare in the corporate world. The IPO, specifically, opened me up to other parts of the company. After you go public and raise millions, there are new business ventures to invest in, and the first people to run them get plucked from the inside. That was my in.

The year was a turning point for me. Whenever anyone asks how I eventually made the transition from lawyer to CEO, the answer is Bob and money. Bob's greatest strength as a leader was that he was incredibly supportive early on. He gave me opportunities to grow creatively. He depended on me and valued my advice.

He treated me as if I was just as important as—or more important than—the men in the room. He never made me or any of the female executives feel left out. If Bob was taking some colleagues to a Redskins game, then we were *all* going—not just the guys. He was a mentor *and* sponsor in the truest sense, more supportive than any other boss I'd had. Every year Bob would host a fancy five-course dinner at the tony Forest Hills mansion he'd built. At one such gathering, Bob stood up with a glass of champagne in hand. Jeff shot me a look from across the room like he always did, and Randy, who was sitting next to me, squeezed my knee. What was Bob going to say now? Were we going to start another magazine (by then I had three) or maybe a skin care line?

Instead of giving us more work to do, our boss went around the table and said a few kind words about each one of the executives there. He knew how to make you feel special, valued, and seen. When he got to me, Bob said, "And then, of course, there's Debra, the conscience of the company." I was floored. The two of us were always locking horns about the risks he wanted to take that I was sure would bankrupt us. But in that moment, I knew he'd been listening all along. He recognized that I was always trying to do the right thing for the company. Comments like that kept me going.

He never once held me back. He never questioned my commitment after having children and becoming a mom. Heck, the man gave me more work to do. The moment I got back from maternity leave, my career began to take off in ways I had never imagined. So again, I say to women in the workplace, never let "them" (your boss, your colleagues, your competition) convince you that being a mother will be a drag on your ambition. It won't. But it will change things. It will force you to take a hard look at your priorities and the support network surrounding you. What you see won't always be good. It took me far too long to realize that I had to staff up my home life just as I did new businesses. I couldn't run a magazine or a house alone. At one point in my career, I had four people working in my house. The extra help was a privilege most women in the workforce don't have. So how do they manage? I still say find the support system—whether that means moving close to or in with family or having your partner's career take a back seat. Either way there have to be adjustments and hard decisions made if you want to buck the system and climb to the top of the ranks as a female executive. Because, yes, you are still bucking the system. But what I want you to know is that it is possible.

There was a time, not too long before the IPO, when I was convinced the opposite was true—that there would always be a low ceiling for women, especially mothers.

Six weeks after I had Quinn, a major legal meeting was scheduled in New York with the global music licensing company BMI. BET had been going back and forth with their legal department for what seemed like an eternity on fees for the music we played on air. It was a yearslong battle that could absolutely wait until I returned from maternity leave in a few short months. But BMI insisted the meeting stay on the books and that I be there.

"But I just had a C-section," I told the outside counsel BET had hired to represent us in the negotiations.

"They're not budging," he told me over the phone. In truth, this was a major negotiation that would affect BET for a long time to come. BMI had ignored us for years, but now that BET was expanding its audience and settling into music-forward programming, the licensing company wanted its cut, and it didn't want to wait one more day to get the deal hammered out. "You're general counsel, Debra. You've got to be there." I was still the bulk of legal department, and there was no one to pass the responsibility on to. Randy thought the whole thing was nuts. "Don't they have phones in New York? Why can't they conference you in?" This is where being indispensable goes wrong.

There was no way around it. I packed my breast pump, kissed my six-week-old baby goodbye, and boarded the US Air shuttle to New York still not fully recovered from the major surgery I'd had to bring my son safely into the world. I'd never been away from him for more than a couple of hours, and as a new mom I had no clue what to expect. As soon as the plane left the runway, I felt the let-down reflex, that familiar tingle that means milk is on the way. *Oh no*, I thought, *not already*. By the time we arrived in Manhattan and I caught a cab to our outside counsel's Midtown headquarters, my breasts were as hard as rocks. Breast milk leaking through my white shirt was not an option. I had to pump and fast.

Hustling through the law firm's doors, I immediately spotted my counsel and the licensing company's six lawyers waiting for me in a fishbowl conference room on display. I didn't spare them more than a glance through the glass walls as I made a beeline for the female receptionist. "Where is your bathroom?" I asked her without a hello. She pointed, and I headed in that direction.

Tears streamed down my face as I crouched in a bathroom stall while the men were in the conference room, unbuttoned my blouse, attached the pump to my throbbing breast, and squeezed. Pain fired through my chest. I kept going, emptying one breast entirely and then the other. The milk—liquid gold—went down the toilet. I splashed a bit of cool water from the sink onto my face and then walked back the meeting room. "Good afternoon, gentlemen," I said with a tight smile as I took my seat. No one ever knew but me (and maybe that receptionist).

On my way back to DC, I passed a Toys"R"Us in the same building and dipped in to buy Quinn the biggest Raggedy Andy doll I'd ever seen. The child was six weeks old, but I had to do something that day to feel like a good mom. I'd been an excellent executive, but my motherhood tank that day was low. Of course, that meeting never should've happened. I should've pushed back more. I was on maternity leave. They could have waited. But I felt backed into a corner, and that familiar "good girl," do-as-you're-told sensibility was creeping back up. I didn't want motherhood to stop me from being the best, but what I didn't know then was that I didn't have anything to prove. And more importantly, these men didn't care about me—Debra Lee. They cared about bottom lines, contracts, and fee structures. It didn't matter that I had every reason not to be in that meeting. Was this what I had worked so hard for? Was this what success looked like? Crying in a bathroom stall over literal spilled milk?

BET's meteoric rise set off by the IPO didn't leave me any room to contemplate the deeper questions. Questions we should all be asking ourselves when it comes to work–life balance, whether you're trying to juggle a marriage, children, aging parents, or simply more time to yourself. What does success look like? What are your passions? What is your purpose? And how do all three of those concepts align with how you live your life and spend your time? For me, the excitement of learning and leading new parts of the business was enough to keep me going—and to take on more. BET was the first job that I ever had where I wasn't thinking about what my next job would be. Every other position had been a ladder rung to the next level up, but when I got to BET, as hard as it was in the beginning, it just felt like this was where I was supposed to be. And if this company was where I belonged, then I wanted to know every nook and cranny of it. I wanted to immerse myself in the business and soak up all that I could.

It was a completely different career path than the one I'd envisioned back at Brown or even Harvard. Outside of making partner at a Big Law firm, being the general counsel of a company was the pinnacle of an attorney's career. There was no more up from there. After practicing law for just five years, I felt incredibly accomplished and proud of my GC title at BET. But the more business responsibilities I took on, the further I got from my legal duties—and I liked it. And Bob was all too happy to oblige.

I know I keep ringing this bell, but I never wanted to be a lawyer. Working at the magazine was creatively freeing in a way that I didn't know I needed. It also fulfilled a childhood dream that I'd locked away since arriving at Brown so many years before. While I was a senior at Dudley High, I wrote a column about our school's goings-on for the *Carolina Peacemaker*, Greensboro's local Black newspaper. Turning in my copy of "Dudley Scene" every week made me feel powerful then, as if I truly had a voice that was worth reading. I loved it and had every intention of studying journalism in college. But Brown did not have a journalism department, so I reached for Chinese Communist Ideology instead. The dream never died though. I kept it in my back pocket as I pursued the interests that paid. But the lesson here isn't simply "don't give up on your dreams." It's the meantime that counts. If you do great work in the job you have, then when the opportunity for the job you want comes around, your name will be one of the first in the ring. Trust me. Bob knew he wanted me to be publisher of the magazines from the beginning. The job was mine because I had a proven track record of success.

* * *

Putting out a magazine every month brought me back to those days back in Greensboro, thinking up new column ideas in my bedroom in Benbow Park. The work was just so much more interesting than preparing formal legal documents or fighting people over contract disputes at BET. I'd always been a creative at heart, and the magazines woke that side of me up after years of neglect. I had a young staff that was passionate about the work, and spending time with them was like a jolt of energy each week. I didn't just love it, I needed it. At one point I was running three BET magazines: *YSB, Emerge,* and *BET Weekend,* a newspaper insert much like *Parade.* Sitting in on story pitch meetings with Frank and his team of hungry writers was inspiring. *This,* I thought, *is what BET can do. We can provide opportunities for young creatives that wouldn't exist otherwise. We can tell stories no one tells.* Working with the magazines plugged me back into my passion, filling me up with the same inspiration I'd felt when I'd first walked into the BET offices. I hatched a plan to make that job my only job.

"Just make me the publisher of the magazine division and hire someone else to replace me as general counsel," I told Bob over a lunch meeting at the Four Seasons. He didn't look up from his steak.

"Absolutely not."

"There are a *ton* of smart Black lawyers in town. This is DC. I'm not the only one," I said. "We can easily find someone great."

"Oh no, no," replied Bob. "I trust *you*, Debi. You. No one else. I don't want anybody else in that position."

My heart sank. This was familiar, this feeling of being trapped in a position that no longer served me as it once had. I was stuck. After seven years as the head of the legal department, I was no longer inspired by the role that had once been so exciting. I had a choice to make. BET was my home, but the walls were closing in. Leaving wasn't on my radar—then. I just wanted to find a way to stay at the company I loved, do the work I loved, and feel good about it instead of feeling stretched paper-thin. Sinking my teeth into the business side of BET meant taking on more responsibilities, more time away from my family. What would make the long nights, extra work, and added stress worth it? The short answer was money. In my mind, getting a bigger paycheck would make the added workload (and motherlode) even out. I didn't want much, just a 5 to 10 percent raise, which would signify that the powers that be (read: Bob) not only recognized but rewarded the fact that I was doing much more than my job description.

Remember from the beginning, Bob had made it crystal clear to all the executive vice presidents that he paid everybody the same. We all started at $50,000 and received the same yearly bonuses and salary increases. I'd taken a hefty pay cut to join BET with the promise of more money to come as the company grew. But that was many years and many new job titles ago. Because the senior executives weren't gifted stock before the company went public, we were all still working our tails off for the same semi-decent salaries. Plus, I was juggling several other roles on top of my demanding job as general counsel. While it had a nice egalitarian ring to it, paying us the same was in no way fair.

I said all this at a compensation committee meeting with Bob, Ty Brown, and Herb Wilkins. By then not only was I general counsel and publisher, but also I was the head of business development and strategy, overseeing all the new ventures the company was putting its brand on. Heck, I'd soon spend a year of my life strategizing how to open a BET casino in Las Vegas. Bob wanted BET to be *the* Black brand in America, dominating every aspect of our consumers' lives. If he had his way, our customers would wake up and turn on BET and then open their local newspaper to read *BET Weekend* while wearing a BET jogging suit. Later they might grab lunch at BET on Jazz or dinner at BET Soundstage. Vacationers could party at BET's nightclub at Disney World in Orlando or gamble at our hotel partnership. And they'd pay for it all with their trusted BET Visa.

"Gentlemen, this isn't about the money," I told them. "This is about value and recognition. I have three titles here. As head of business development alone, I'm overseeing a dozen possible ventures. I can do the work and do it well. We all know that. But let's not ignore the fact that the work is more than demanding. Doesn't that deserve acknowledgment?" I asked, immensely proud of the fact that I got through my speech without my voice cracking too much. I'd practiced countless times in the mirror before that lunch. Randy, who'd been taking on more and more at home as my profile at work rose, said I was ready. "You got this," he told me that morning. But it wasn't enough.

Herb, one of Bob's best friends and a board member of BET's parent company, told me that there were a ton of lawyers in DC who would kill for my job, throwing the same reasoning I'd given Bob months before right back in my face. "If you don't like what Bob pays you," he said, "then you should probably just leave."

Well, I thought after splashing cool water on my face in the ladies' room, starring down my own reflection in the mirror after a quick cry, *he hasn't said nothing but a word.* Leave? It sounded like a sentence, the verdict after giving years of my life to the company. But if working at BET had taught me anything, it was that respect was a two-way street. I deserved it, and they weren't giving it to me.

CHAPTER SEVEN

FEELING UNDERVALUED

This is the story of how I went from plotting my escape from corporate America to becoming the first chief operating officer of BET, positioning myself to one day be CEO. All that happened within a year. But to appreciate just how steep the climb was, you have to understand why I was ready to leave in the first place. It wasn't one thing; it was many. Alarm bells had been ringing loud and clear for years, alerting me in no uncertain terms that I was overworked and underappreciated. But I consistently ignored those flashing red lights in favor of rolling my sleeves up and being "the good girl" my dad always taught me to be. Work hard, then harder, and wait for the reward even when all signs are pointing toward the door. Don't do that. Don't ignore that gut feeling. I did for far too long, and while success was waiting for me on the other side, I was almost too worn out to make it there.

By 1992, I had hit my stride at the company. The IPO was wildly successful, *YSB* magazine was doing well, and Randy and I had reliable childcare. But, of course, resting on our laurels was not the BET way. The company was doing too well, so it was time for a shake-up. Like clockwork, it wasn't long before Bob called a surprise senior staff meeting (he loved doing that) because he had a huge announcement to make. "What do you think it is this time?" someone asked as the group of us made our way past the lobby tree to our glass conference room. "He probably wants to buy Johnson Publishing," I said only half-joking. That would be a Bob move.

"Okay, I know you're all curious, so let me get right down to it," said Bob from the head of the table. "You all have been working nonstop. We see it. We appreciate it. And we figure you could use a break. So the entire executive team is going to the South of France for two weeks, all expenses paid." We might as well have been in a football stadium, the cheers were that loud. The senior team and their spouses were going to Europe. It was extravagant, classy, and just what the overworked team needed. That was the thing about Bob. He had impeccable timing and always knew when and just how much love to give. Whether it was long-overdue appreciation or extra points on a deal, Bob was a master conductor. Sure, we loved to talk junk about him during long lunches at Houston's, especially when he had another swing-for-the-fences idea that would mean longer hours for us. But the man knew how to make you feel appreciated, loved even. I was busy planning my outfits in my head when the catch came. The *whole* team couldn't go. Someone had to stay back and man the ship. Guess who? Debi can do it. Ring, ring, ring. This was an alarm.

I should've been disappointed, frustrated, something. But instead

I felt proud, happy even, that Bob would put me in charge of the company. It meant that I could be trusted to step into Bob's shoes without so much as a blink from anyone. Running the company for two weeks while the entire senior team was off cruising the Riviera and sipping champagne from actual Champagne? Sure, no problem.

When the group got back—looking well rested, tanned, and happy—Bob offered me a consolation prize. The 1992 Summer Olympics were a few months away in Barcelona. "How about an all-expenses-paid trip for just you and Randy?" he asked in the middle of a one-on-one debrief on how the company fared while everyone was away. See? He had great timing. There was one potential problem, though. I'd just found out that I was pregnant again. Randy and I were elated. Quinn was two, and it seemed like the right time to make him a big brother. After checking with my OB/GYN, who gave me the go-ahead, I told Bob's assistant to book our trip.

We left Quinn with my mom, who was all too happy to spend some quality time with her grandbaby ("Just two weeks, right, y'all?"), and then proceeded to have the time of our lives in Spain with only a slight twinge of guilt. The time alone was necessary medicine. Randy and I had been running on E with no end in sight. Even though we'd managed to make it work, the break from our day-to-day hustle was a godsend. Any married couple with a young child and two demanding jobs would agree. We started in Barcelona for the Games, walking down the tree-lined and buzzing Las Ramblas hand in hand and sans any responsibilities. Then we decided to ditch the touristy crowds and head south to the beach town Marbella. The two of us were in the stands watching a bullfight when I noticed the blood in my seat. "Something's wrong," I told my husband, panicked. "Let's call the doctor," he replied, squeezing my hand.

Dr. Hicks suggested I get checked out at the local hospital before we jumped to any conclusions. "This might just be some normal first-trimester spotting," he said, trying to soothe the terrified pregnant lady on the other end. Through a translator, the Spanish doctor at the tiny two-story hospital in town confirmed the worst. I was having a miscarriage. Randy wouldn't let go of my hand as the tears came. I wanted nothing more than to get home immediately to hug my son and to mourn the loss of the child we were just dreaming about. "That's way too dangerous, Debi," Dr. Hicks told us over the phone in the cramped examination room. "You could risk hemorrhaging on the plane or worse." Before we could safely fly home, our doctor advised that I get a dilation and curettage procedure (D&C) right away. I was scared to death.

We were in a remote resort town. No one spoke English, and Randy couldn't be in the room with me during the procedure. I was terrified and alone. To cope, I disassociated, turning the whole horrible affair into an out-of-body experience. Everything was a blur. I can draw up few memories from the time Randy left the room until he came back to stroke my hair and wipe my tears. There was a nurse with a kind face who came in to shave me. The room where the procedure was performed was hellishly hot. The windows flung open wide. Flies buzzed in my ears as the doctor and I struggled to communicate. Then it was over, and as soon as it was safe, Randy and I got on a plane back to Washington. The entire flight I felt jittery, almost unhinged. "Debi? Debi? You okay?" my husband asked, already knowing the answer. Of course I wasn't okay. We weren't. We'd lost our baby. The ache was like nothing I'd ever felt before; nothing felt right. But instead of saying all that, I spent the next six hours pacing up and down the aisles, trying to escape the heartache.

That Monday I went back to work like nothing had happened. It was so early in my pregnancy that no one knew we were expecting. It had been a sweet little secret between Randy and me, which also meant that the grief was ours alone to bear. I took zero time off to mourn, taking my maxim about working at BET—"absolutely no downtime"—to the extreme. I jumped right back into it. The work, which was ratcheting up as the company diversified its business portfolio, was something of a balm. It distracted me from what was going on inside by zeroing in on what was in front of me—more contracts to approve, deals to negotiate, businesses to acquire. I relished the exhaustion, which allowed me to pretend like the miscarriage never happened.

"How was Spain?" Bob asked my first week back from our "vacation." "I hope you got some R and R because a hotel wants to partner with us on a BET-branded casino. We might need to head to Vegas later this week. What do you think?"

"Sounds like a plan, Bob," I said without looking up from my notepad. If Bob heard the sadness in my voice, he didn't let on. He offered me work, and I happily accepted it, hoping to drown out the pain in an ocean of paperwork and waves of meetings.

This was another alarm bell that I ignored. It marked the start of a pattern of pushing myself to the brink and using my work as a kind of painkiller. It was a toxic trap that would continue much too long into my tenure at the company. A dangerous pit I don't want other women to fall into. It was my choice to dive in then because I didn't see another way past my trauma. Taking weeks off to heal physically and emotionally was a necessity I viewed as a luxury. The mix-up cost me. Sure, the work was getting done, but in my office with the door closed, I was on edge, unfocused, and, at times, frightened. The grief hadn't gone anywhere. It was hiding under my desk. I thought work was helping me get over my loss, but I needed a different kind of help. I should have been up front about what my family was going through. I should have found a therapist and sat on her couch before ever setting foot back into my office. Work became my faulty measuring stick, responsible for gauging how well I was doing overall. If things were going great at the office, then I was doing okay. Work is not a refuge. Find your refuge.

Joy finally started to color my days again when I found out I was pregnant with our daughter Ava six months later. But there was a cloud. I was 39, and my pregnancy was considered "risky," especially after the miscarriage. The invasive tests and extra appointments served as a reminder that once again hope could be snatched away at any moment. It was a stressful 40 weeks. But I was going to accept all the help I could get this time around. So when we brought Ava home from the hospital, my mom, a nanny, and a housekeeper were part of the team. None of that made being a mom of two and an executive times three a cakewalk. Breastfeeding was a nightmare. Ava couldn't figure out how to latch, and my poor nipples were raw from the battle. We spent a small fortune on lactation consultants until my mother convinced me it was time for formula. "You tried your best, baby," she assured me. It took weeks before we found a brand Ava could keep down without vomiting. Meanwhile I still had to hop on a conference call or two with a hungry baby hollering in the background, but I cared much less about what the men on the other line might think. Ava's arrival was another alarm. She made me slow down—ever so slightly—and assess what lay ahead of me in life and in the office.

From my first day at BET, I'd worked like a woman with something to prove because back then I did have something to prove. The leap from associate to general counsel was a big one,

one that everyone around me (my bosses at the firm, my dad) had questioned ostensibly because BET was so new. But maybe there was more to it? Was it because I was so young? Because I was a woman? While I never once gave those creeping thoughts a voice outside my head, my all-systems-go approach to work was in part because of those doubts. Impostor syndrome comes for us all.

But by the time Ava came around, I'd proven the point 10 times over. I was good at my job. So good, in fact, that Bob kept giving me more jobs to do. I was done with adding self-doubt to that pile. Women get caught in that trap of insecurity much too easily. We question our credentials while holding more distinguished degrees than anyone else at the boardroom table. We question our ability to take on the bigger title, despite doing all the work required without the change on the nameplate. We question our very commitment as the clock strikes midnight and we're still plugging away. I remember when that last point finally hit home for me. The precise moment when I realized that I was doing more work and that no one—especially the men in the room—was going to pat me on the back for it.

It all started because someone else had dropped the ball.

Remember, 1992 was the year of my career renaissance. The successful IPO that I helped launch was a turning point. But I never took a break because I was still too terrified to take my foot off the gas. My biggest source of anxiety? BET's chief financial officer, Antonia Duncan. In my opinion, and I was not alone, the woman was not up to her job, and as the point person for all things financial, that was major. It seemed that to cover up the fact that she didn't know much about the complicated ins and outs of the company's financial future, Antonia's strategy during her rocky tenure was to point the finger at other executives. The woman chastised this one executive for being over budget more times than I can count, going so far as to accuse him of stealing. "There are a lot of irregularities in your budget reports," she said in her Panamanian lilt during a senior meeting. The man was so livid he could hardly speak. Instead he calmly got up from the conference table and we all watched as this six-foot-four executive in an electric blue suit punted his expensive leather briefcase clear across the conference room. He could no longer take it. Antonia even came for me once. During my first few months at the company, I noticed my paycheck had been docked. When I asked her about it, Antonia said, "Well, you've been clocking out for hours during the workday." I was stunned. "I'm going to the law library. We don't have enough legal reference tools in the office." And she had the nerve to respond, "Debra, I have no way of knowing whether or not you're doing work outside of this building." As a professional, I had never been disrespected over my office hours. I was not an hourly worker.

Fast-forward years later to the public offering and all the financial scrutiny that came with it. We were on a routine call with the Wall Street analysts whose job it was to assess the company's financial health quarterly. And our CFO was running point. I was nervous the entire time, hoping that she knew enough to make her way through. We weren't so lucky. After the IPO, during one of our first quarterly analyst calls, there was a question about a discrepancy between BET's internal subscriber count versus the estimate that Nielsen, the media data giant, was projecting. Black TV programmers *always* had a bone to pick with Nielsen because the company did not have a diverse enough sample size to properly measure Black viewership. Antonia should have been able to easily explain all that to the finance guys, but she couldn't. And just like that Wall Street lost confidence in the company. That day BET stock took a nosedive from $25 per share to $12 by the closing bell. The board was having a heart attack. Bob called the NYSE himself and halted trading of BET stock. The entire Georgetown office was in crisis mode. "Debra, we need you," Bob called from his top-floor office where he, Herb Wilkins, and myself would be holed up for the next five hours. I passed Antonia's office on my way up the spiral staircase, worried about all the extra work we needed to do.

This was the kind of mistake that kept me, as general counsel, up all night. The kind of mistake that gave me nightmares. The kind of mistake I had been killing myself at work to avoid at all costs. But no matter who held the blame, I was still the one left holding the bag in the end. Were all the hand-wringing and extra stress I took on worth it? In that moment I didn't have time to decide because the company needed me. We had to discuss strategy, schedule more calls with the board, square the subscriber numbers, get on another call with the Wall Street analysts, and more. Catastrophes are inevitable in business. It's not if, it's when. Making yourself crazy trying to avoid them is a fool's errand. I could work myself to the ground or I could give myself room—either way there would come a time when we all would have to huddle up in Bob's office till almost midnight to fix what someone else broke. It was a necessary lesson in letting go that would take me a few more years to truly understand. But the seed had been planted.

—

"A lot of other people would love to do this job." Herb's words had been playing nonstop on a loop in my head since my disastrous compensation meeting. The alarm bells had been telling me for years that I deserved more money, but when I'd asked for it, these three men responded in unison with a loud no. It was time to let go.

The morning after, I climbed into the shower hoping that the warm water would help wash away the sinking feeling in my gut. The tears came once again. It was like a death. I knew I had to leave. I couldn't pour my heart and soul into a company that wouldn't give me $5,000 more a year. I didn't simply want to leave, I had to. After nine years, I had hit a wall. The only way to move forward was to bulldoze right through it.

Leaving isn't just hard, it can hurt. Especially when you've poured so much of yourself into a company that it no longer feels like a job but a part of who you are. Quitting is akin to losing a limb. BET was a place where I had felt seen and heard. Where this shy Southern girl got to grow and expand beyond what she thought was possible, tapping into so many facets of herself. I'd become a creative, an executive, a mentor, a leader. What other company could compare? Where else could I work where I might be sitting down with Denzel Washington explaining corporate board responsibilities one minute and the next signing off on *YSB*'s May cover girl—Jada Pinkett Smith? It was a dream job in every sense. And, sure, Bob was a demanding boss, but he was also my biggest cheerleader. "Debi can do it" was a challenge I constantly rose to not only meet but exceed. But was the nonstop stress worth it? Missing Quinn's first steps. Not getting to tuck Ava in at night. Climbing into bed next to my exhausted husband after midnight. For the first time in my career, the answer was clear.

━━

"That should do it, babe. You're all set up," said Randy after installing new business planning software on our computer at home.

"So I just plug away at this thing and then poof, out pops my plan?" I said with our infant daughter Ava bouncing on my lap and pawing at the keyboard.

"Well, all the ideas come from you," said Randy, smiling. "And we know that won't be a problem." Was I really going to do this? I was going to leave BET and start my own business?

The decision didn't come lightly. But just thinking about it made me lighter. I could even see it on Randy's face. All the extra hours in the office and on the road had taken their toll. I could feel the pressure building in my marriage.

Randy never complained, but the tension between us was undeniable. My work was affecting our marriage. My husband was supportive, but he didn't sign up to be a single dad on the nights and weekends. He wanted his wife and partner around. A lot of the family stuff was falling on his shoulders—doctor's appointments, drop-off and pick-up, dinner, everything—while I was zipping around the country with Bob pitching new businesses to investors or touring a clothing factory. BET had started a design studio and a fashion line called Xto24-7. "Are we married to that name?" I asked Bob, trying to be diplomatic in our brainstorming meeting instead of saying what I really thought: *That's so dumb.* "You are not the target market for this stuff," Bob responded dismissively. That was the logic he often used whenever I or the other executives pushed back on his wilder ideas. Like the time Bob announced that he'd been contemplating licensing old *Amos 'n' Andy* reruns from CBS.

"What? No way," said Jeff with a laugh. Even he didn't think Bob would go so far as to buy one of the most racially contentious TV shows of the 21st century. *Amos 'n' Andy* began as a radio show created by and starring two white men who, in the racist minstrel tradition, played two Black men. CBS aired the TV adaptation starring Black men in the titular stereotypical roles from 1951 through 1953. While the series was canceled after pressure from the NAACP, it ran in syndication for more than a decade.

"You can't be serious," added Curtis, who usually gave our boss the benefit of the doubt.

"Our audience will never go for it," I said. My dad never let my siblings and me tune into *Amos 'n' Andy* growing up. The grotesque and negative stereotypes the 1950s sitcom promoted made it unwatchable in our house. "The phones will be ringing off the hook!"

Bingo! That's exactly what Bob wanted. More controversy meant more attention, which translated into bigger ratings and an increase in subscribers. We all knew this was Bob's well-worn tactic, but this was also BET. Weren't we better than that?

"Think of the historic significance," said Bob, playing devil's advocate, one of the man's favorite roles. CBS, which had locked *Amos 'n' Andy* away decades before, was reluctant to give Bob the keys to the vault. But, as always, he had his ways, convincing the network execs there that BET was the perfect place to shed light on the racial and cultural issues of the time. We aired a panel discussion about stereotypical images in the media after broadcasting two episodes of the show. There was even a 1-800 number viewers could call to vote on whether the channel should show more. It was a resounding no from practically everyone who tuned in, definitely not the ratings bonanza Bob thought it would be. Years later I suggested we buy the two seasons of *Frank's Place* about a professor who ends up back home in New Orleans running his family's restaurant.

"It's too expensive," said Bob when I brought it up. At $20,000, it was about double the price of what we would normally pay for a syndicated program, but the show was so good I thought we could stretch the budget a little.

"People will love it. Tim and Daphne Reid are great, and it's written so smartly."

"Debra, you and your Ivy League friends are not the BET audience." I resented that. I knew our audience just as well as Bob—or at least I thought I did. He was right. The ratings for our broadcast of *Frank's Place* were terrible. I didn't make programming suggestions again until over a decade later when I took over as CEO. But Bob never let that stumble shake my confidence or his. What I learned about business in those days was that failure was not a bad thing; in fact, failure didn't even exist. Business was all about taking risks. If one idea didn't pan out the way you thought it would, you learned from it, wrote it off, and moved on to the next big swing. Nowhere was that more evident than when the company was flush with cash from the public offering. We had millions to invest and we took lots of risks.

The business of the cable channel was surprisingly less and less important. "We've got that formula down," Bob would say. He didn't want to sink much more into the channel; instead, the proceeds from the IPO were used to grow the brand. His theory was that if anything happened with the cable industry, the company would have diverse revenue streams to fall back on, and the BET brand was so strong you could put it on other things. Despite being overworked, what I learned during those years was like free business school. So when it was time for me to leave the company, a light bulb went off. With all the new businesses that I had helped develop at BET, I could start my own.

Use the company, don't let it use you. My advice to anyone who wants to move up the ladder and eventually earn more is to take on more responsibility first. There are people new to the corporate world who expect to be paid what they are worth immediately. And I get it. No one wants to be undervalued. We're all looking for validation in life, work, and love. But business doesn't always work that way. In fact, the "pay me now" mentality can work against you if all employers see when they look at you is dollar signs. What you want them to see is you—your work, your dedication, your drive. You. That might mean showing and proving, taking on more responsibility without the immediate added income in order to prove your point.

In most scenarios, the money will come when you've proved your value. No smart company invested in its own growth—its people—would risk losing a dedicated and productive employee over a paycheck. That's just bad business. So it *shouldn't* take long. But, of course, as women, we know it can and it does. When that happens—and it definitely will at some point in your career—have an exit strategy in place. Use all that added responsibility, gained knowledge, and one-of-a-kind experience to invest in yourself. You'll be in a position to leave without looking back.

I knew my worth and what Bob, Herb, and Ty were offering—nothing—wasn't going to do it for me. I'd done the research. I knew the salary range for just one of the positions I had much less all three combined. The little 5 to 10 percent raise I'd worked up the courage to ask for was more symbolic than anything. But for me the pay raise wasn't only about the money. Bob was leaning heavily on me. I was being taken advantage of, and I deserved more. I knew it, they knew it, and they still had the nerve to say no. All of that together was like a neon sign flashing TIME TO GO. My grand plan? Start a toy store.

There was a sweet mom-and-pop shop in Chevy Chase where every parent in Northwest Washington would stop on their way to a birthday party. With my insane schedule, I was always there about 15 minutes before the party started, whizzing through the aisles for the latest Beanie Baby or Bop It. I'd dash through its doors stressed and frazzled thinking about some task left undone back at the office, but once I was in the aisles surrounded by bright colors, buzzing toys, and beautiful dolls, I felt calmer. Quinn and Ava loved it there, of course. Seeing their faces light up whenever I told them we were headed to the toy store for a quick stop always made me smile. It was our happy place, and who doesn't want to spend all day at their happy place? At the toy store, I was joy-filled.

"I want to open my own toy store," I told Randy over our kitchen table one evening after the kids had gone to bed. Life at home had gotten slightly easier with daycare for Quinn and a nanny for Ava, but no one can do it like Mom. My absence was still keenly felt. The long nights hadn't slowed down. Starting a business would be grueling. I knew that from all my experience. But this would be mine. I could make my own hours, spend more time with the kids. Be present. I told Randy all this over a glass of good wine, and my husband didn't bat an eye.

"What do you need?" That's how I ended up with business planning software on my Mac a week later. Randy was ready. One weekend I caught the train to Manhattan to attend the American International Toy Fair. The Jacob K. Javits Convention Center was packed with trade professionals and retailers from across the country. I even visited showrooms in the city to clock trends and meet more people in the business. This was happening. I was not playing.

Shockingly I wasn't even scared about striking out on my own. It seemed like the smartest next step. Even my dad's voice in the back of my head—"Is this what you went to law school for?"— couldn't stop me. The answer I'd tell my father was yes, I'd done everything right. I'd been in the front seat of a business success story, and all that time and work put in meant that I had the privilege of choice. And I choose myself and my family. I made my mind up to go and that was it. There was just one drawback to leaving that tugged at me more than a little: Bob.

Quitting BET meant that we wouldn't see one another anymore. Bob had become a good friend and a mentor at work and in life over the near decade that we'd been working together. I was going to miss our conversations and his advice. When I stopped to think about what I was giving up—*Bob wouldn't be my boss*—I was surprised about how keenly that loss hit me.

While the higher-ups knew how unhappy I was, they never suspected that I planned to leave, despite Herb's threats. No one at the company knew I'd been mapping out my own business for months. Moving in silence is your best bet. It allows you to play both sides until you're ready to pick one. So, while I was negotiating (and failing) to get more money at BET, I was using the incredible business knowledge I'd gained to forge my next path. Bob didn't help matters; it was like our conversation about my salary had never happened. He didn't bring it up again until the two of us were on a business trip in South Africa.

Secretary of Commerce Ron Brown was hosting a conference in South Africa to promote trade relations and introduce Black business leaders to their counterparts on the continent. Bob wanted to use the trip to explore more opportunities for BET, and I was there as his support person. It hit me during the flight to Johannesburg from London that this could be the last business trip I took with Bob and BET. "Debra, you look contemplative," Bob remarked as I took in the clouds outside the window. "Here, listen to this," he said, offering me one of his earphones to hear some music he'd been playing. I hesitated at first. The gesture seemed familiar, intimate even. But I took it, and for the rest of the flight, we listened to jazz together.

"What salary do you see yourself making in life?" Bob asked while the two of us were out at dinner in a fancy hotel in Joburg. I had my business plan for Lee's Toy Store completed on my computer. All that was left was for me to print it out and set my plan into motion. I could no longer work as hard as I did and still make the same thing that everyone else made. I threw out a number that sounded big.

"Just a million?" Bob asked with a smirk, and I knew then that something was brewing in that mind of his. I just didn't know what.

"Would you ever consider being COO?"

"Is that even on the table?" I asked, stunned. In truth I'd never thought about it because BET was Bob's company; naming a number two would mean that he actually planned to hand over the keys to the kingdom one day, and giving up control was not something Robert L. Johnson did. It was the prevailing wisdom around the office that Bob was going to run the company until the day he died. So the details of his succession weren't important. But in the end, Bob wanted BET to last. He wanted his business legacy to continue, and his kids were too young to bring into the fold. In order for him to expand his own corporate interests outside the cable business, he had to hand over the reins to someone eventually.

Plus, as we all know, I was indispensable, and Bob knew it.

He also knew I was unhappy, although just how unhappy I'd made sure to keep close to the vest. From a leadership strategy perspective, offering me the title of COO was a brilliant chess move. The position consolidated all the work I'd already been doing. It also justified Bob paying me more since the title of heir apparent to the throne demanded it. The role even provided future opportunities for me to learn more about the business as a whole, from programming to advertising to day-to-day operations. Instead of running a team of about 80 people between the magazines and the business development staff, I would now oversee all 500 of the company's employees.

"Why? I don't do programming. And then, of course, there's my 'Ivy League' taste," I said. Bob laughed.

"I don't want a programmer. I want someone with a business mind, someone who knows the risks, who'll keep us in check. Someone who doesn't go gaga over seeing a celebrity. Although you did enjoy that Denzel meeting," he said with a smile.

"There are a lot of guys on the team who've been with you since the beginning who would want this," I said, talking myself into it while talking Bob out of it.

"You're right, there are. And they've asked," he said. For his part, Bob got to keep me on, step out of the swamp of daily operations, focus on his other interests, and avoid playing favorites among his buddies on the senior team. The man was offering me a pair of golden handcuffs.

"Debra?"

"Thank you, Bob. I'd be honored." And I was honored but also shocked and so happy I was practically giddy. I would cement my new passion for the business side of the company and—this was important—finally get to hire my own general counsel. The mere thought of shedding my legal work once and for all after 14 years as a working lawyer felt like a rebirth. That's what I had been looking forward to as a toy store owner—a renewal of passion and purpose. This promotion was it.

After the two of us got back from South Africa, the entire senior team headed to Arizona for our annual executive retreat. No one knew he'd offered me the COO position. On the first night of our retreat, Bob gifted everyone the book *Built to Last: Successful Habits of Visionary Companies* by James C. Collins and Jerry I. Porras. The message was clear from the first page: "The key point is that a visionary company is an organization—an institution. All individual leaders, no matter how charismatic or visionary, eventually die." It was certainly heavy-handed, but Bob's point was made. He was finally ready to establish a line of succession.

I spent the next week drafting my own press release to the company. "You still working on that?" asked Bob, popping his head into my office across the hall from his on the sixth floor. It was the night before we planned to tell the company, and I was beyond nervous. In an instant, I'd be dubbed the next in line. People who I used to work shoulder to shoulder with would now have to report to me. Hundreds of people would be looking to me for answers, leadership, guidance. The promotion was as mental and emotional as it was organizational. I'd have to stretch to meet it, and while I had no doubt that was possible, I also wanted to brace myself for the inevitable growing pains. My assistant Gloria and I stayed in the office until 11 p.m. writing and rewriting that release. Bob had gone home hours before.

The next day Bob gathered the entire company in person and via teleconference at our headquarters in Northeast DC, which sat right next to the soundstage and production studio I had helped build years before. There, Bob announced that he had appointed me COO, which meant that I would be running the company on a daily basis. The room was too stunned to react for a second. Some folks were confused about what was happening. Was Bob leaving? Was BET still his? But once we both made our statements, it was a sign that that we'd be working in concert. "I'm so honored and excited to continue the legacy of this incredible company," I began. That's when the room went wild. The applause was thunderous. As I headed back up the hallway to get to the executive meeting that was to follow the announcement, female employees grasped my hands. "It's so good to see a woman in this role!" "Nice people never win. This is incredible." "Debra, you're going to be amazing."

The contrast between that welcome and what was waiting for me in the executive conference room was stark. There were men sitting around that table who were openly pissed. Walking into that snake pit felt like a slap in the face. Really? You're mad? Have you not seen the amount of work I've put in for the past nine years? Do you honestly think I don't deserve this? Of course, I couldn't say all that as I took my place directly to the right of Bob's seat at the top of the table. "Congratulations, Debra," whispered some of my colleagues. But those weren't nearly as enthusiastic as I would've liked. The other whispers were louder. Why hadn't Jeff gotten it? He'd been head of programming for 20 years. Or what about James Ebron? He was head of media sales. I could see the doubt and dissent growing already. The vibe in that room was only a polite step up from hostile. I knew the transition wouldn't be without its bumps. But this? In that moment, it hit me. These weren't my colleagues anymore or even my friends. The shift felt like a splash of cold water. Outside I had my game face on, but inside I was mourning the loss of camaraderie that had flown out the window the moment Bob named me COO.

"Let me explain," began Bob, which was far from comforting. It was like he was asking for forgiveness. Inside, I groaned. Instead of celebrating, he was explaining. Ugh. "BET is not like most Black media companies. This isn't Johnson Publishing or Black Enterprise. I respect what John and Earl built, but I want this place to last for a *long* time, whether my family is directly involved with running it or not. That's how you create a legacy that's built to last. I wanted a professional manager in this position, and I feel that's Debra. This is not about flash and splashy programming. This is business."

Crickets. Not just awkward silence but a charged silence. That's when Bob turned to me and said something that would damage my ability to lead the company for years.

"Debra, would you step out of the room for a moment?" I turned to face him with a look that said, *You can't be serious.* Bob didn't repeat himself. He just waited for me to get up and walk out of the room. Needless to say, I was not happy about it. Wasn't I COO? Why would I need to step out of the room? The thought of my former friends arguing about my new job instead of toasting me was both infuriating and painful. But mostly infuriating. And don't get me started on Bob! The man had just named me his number two, and he was already undercutting me in front of everybody. How did this bode for the rest of my time at the top? I wanted to scream. I wanted to suck my teeth. I wanted to say, "I don't think so. I'll stay right here," while staring unblinkingly into the faces of all the executives who'd dare question my ability to do the job.

But then I heard a familiar whisper in my ear. *Be a good girl, Debi. Don't rock the boat on your first day.* It was Dad and all the other moments in my life when I'd swallowed my anger in favor of keeping the peace. Even with this new, big, exciting position, I was still the woman who didn't like to make waves. Plus, I'd had the title for all of five seconds. I wasn't about to openly contradict Bob in front of everybody. I could feel my clenched jaw relaxing into a smile anyone with eyes knew was fake. "Okay," I said with a sigh as I walked through the door with my back as straight as a board, and to my office, knowing full well that they were talking about me. I had to sit there alone at my desk for 30 minutes, thinking up all the nasty things they were saying about me in that room. What was this, junior high school? It sure felt like it. I got smacked back to my first months in Greensboro when I was the new girl and the kids at school chased me home throwing rocks. *Why Debi? Does she think she's better than us? She doesn't know anything about programming. She's a lawyer. She isn't ready.* Just when I thought the old self-doubt might drown me, my assistant, Gloria, informed me that the "second meeting" was over. I marched across the hall to Bob's office, an all-dark-wood and cognac-leather affair, to find out what had happened in my absence.

"So?" I asked.

"So?"

"Bob, how'd it go?"

He leaned back in his chair and took me in, perhaps finally feeling the weight of the decision he'd made and what it meant not only for the company but for his own influence. Bob was now not the only one at the very top. The absolute power he held on to for so long was ever so slightly slipping out of his grasp. I think he was at a crossroads. Power was everything to Bob. Did naming me COO mean that he was giving it up? Consolidating? Liberating himself? I don't think he knew the answer himself.

"How'd it go? It went fine. I told them not to worry, you couldn't fire them."

"Why on earth would you tell them that?"

"Because you can't," he said with a blank stare that meant this was a command from my CEO, the only position higher than my own. Noted. Got it. This man wasn't going quietly into the night. He had drawn a line in the sand, singling me out from all his former buddies. To soften the blow of having named not only a number two in the first place but a *female* COO, Bob was sending a very clear message about power and gender. As the next in line, I had power—but only so much. And never more than Bob. The man was still in charge. That was a message for me just as much as it was a message for the guys in the room he'd asked me to leave.

"Look, you saw how it was going in there. Curtis looked ready to chew through concrete. I needed to reassure them that *they* were still part of the team and that only I could change that."

"I don't think that's going to work." Bob had just cut me off at the knees and was acting as if he'd done me a favor. As a corporate manager, you need a stick and a carrot to help incentivize your team to do good and consistent work. The carrot can be bonuses, promotions, praise. The stick is a clear understanding that if you don't do your job well, then you can be fired. Period. Bob took away my stick. That was the first sign that my tenure as COO would be anything but easy.

CHAPTER EIGHT

LESSONS LEARNED

The week before Bob and I left for South Africa—the trip that would forever change the trajectory of my career—a messy coworker delivered a juicy piece of gossip that hadn't landed on my desk yet. See, BET was a warehouse of steamy whisper campaigns. Getting up-to-date on the latest office scuttlebutt was a regular item on everyone's to-do list. Once, I was in the middle of complaining to a trusted colleague about something work-related when he cut me off with this: "You know what your problem is, Debi? You're not sleeping with anyone at work. That makes it all better." What! I gave him a half-hearted punch in the arm and walked away shaking my head. The nerve. Me? Sleep with someone at the company? I was a married woman with two little ones waiting for her at home. The very idea of an office affair was nauseating. I filed it under "Things Debra Would Never," a dusty dossier I didn't crack open again until someone else brought it up years later. Enter the office pot stirrer.

"You know," began this one consultant who had a reputation for throwing grenades and then hiding his hands. From his tone, I knew he was about to tell me something he shouldn't. We were in the middle of an otherwise polite conversation about the schedule for Bob's and my overseas trip when he added ever so nonchalantly, "Everybody thinks you and Bob are having an affair."

"Excuse me," I said, so taken aback that I dipped into the North Carolina drawl usually reserved for close friends and my mom. "What did you say?"

He had the nerve to keep that Cheshire cat grin on his face as he shrugged his shoulders. "I'm just saying. That's the rumor." I didn't dignify it with a response. Bob and me? No way. Sure, the two of us spent an inordinate amount of time together. But CEOs and their senior staff were supposed to be in lockstep—that was the job and the time commitment. Was this just another female executive tax? The entire office assumed that a woman couldn't be in the C-suite without stirring up the suits. It was ridiculous and insulting.

It was a well-worn rumor that Bob had relationships outside his marriage. Rumor had it that he had a girlfriend in several major U.S. cities so when he was traveling for work, which was often, there was always someone available for him to wine and dine. Now that sounded like an exaggeration. But you couldn't put anything past Bob. He also liked to blur the lines a bit between what was inappropriate and what was just for laughs. For years, Bob told the same joke during the sexual harassment discussion (which *he* led) at the BET annual company meeting: "If you're having any issues with your boss harassing you, then be sure to let Debi know. And if Debi is the one doing the harassing, you come talk to me."

Folks would laugh. My cheeks turned fire engine red every time he told it—and he told it every single year.

So was I genuinely surprised by the rumors? I'd like to think I was. But the question mark had been there for longer than I'd care to admit.

Especially after I was named COO and the pair of us traveled together every other week. I tagged along on all Bob's business trips to see firsthand how he carried himself in meetings with investors, potential business partners, and other CEOs. From the outside looking in, I'm sure our trips on the company's private jet to Orlando to negotiate with Disney or Manhattan to talk with fashion brands or Vegas to discuss casinos appeared glamorous, but they *were* real work. Those trips taught me how to negotiate and build partnerships. Bob was the idea man, and I was the executor. He'd make the giant proclamation—"Let's brand a casino"—and then I would follow it up with all the logistics from picking the staff to picking out curtain fabrics for our restaurants. On top of that, I was learning the personalities of the principals we did business with and letting them get to know me. Bob was introducing me to the major players—politicians, bankers, cable operators—as the next in line. When they couldn't get a hold of Bob, they called me. I was soaking up all the knowledge I could before he took his final bow and I became CEO in the future. The timeline for that transition for most number twos is about two years, three tops. It took me ten. Not because *I* wasn't ready. Bob wasn't. I am convinced that not only was he holding on to his title, his position, his power. But he was also holding on to me. Bob didn't want to let me go.

We didn't share our first kiss until six months *after* he appointed me COO. I clung to that fact—that it happened *after*—like a life raft for the next decade as our relationship went from platonic to intimate to toxic and even abusive. Simply writing that last word—*abusive*—feels like a release. It's also terrifying. What will people think—how will my achievements be denied—under the weight of a word like that? It's the reason why I've held in this story and the pain it caused me for so long. But no more. I have the #MeToo movement to thank for that.

On January 1, 2018, I was leafing through the Monday edition of *The New York Times* when a full-page letter announcing the Time's Up movement shook something loose in me.

> … *We have similarly suppressed the violence and demeaning harassment for fear that we will be attacked and ruined in the process of speaking. We share your feelings of anger and shame. We harbor fear that no one will believe us, that we will look weak or that we will be dismissed; and we are terrified that we will be fired or never hired again in retaliation.*

Reading those words brought back memories I'd buried deep. Memories I thought couldn't hurt me anymore. My first thought was "How did they know?" and my second was "I wish I'd called Nina!" A powerful entertainment lawyer I'd known for years, Nina Shaw was helping spearhead the Time's Up campaign in Los Angeles. That year I had just moved to the West Coast from Washington and had been meaning to phone Nina for months and tell her my story. But I never reached out. The idea of divulging what had happened to me was paralyzing. Repeating the words I read in the paper to myself—*We share your feelings of anger and shame*—felt like a mantra. The strength and comfort they offered eventually led me to my first Time's Up meeting. That's how I ended up walking into the Creative Artists Agency's building in

Beverly Hills on a random workday alongside actress Natalie Portman. But it would take another two years before I could muster enough courage to actually speak at a meeting.

At that second meeting, the group focused on a soon-to-be-released documentary about Russell Simmons, *On the Record*, which centered on allegations of harassment and abuse against the hip-hop pioneer. Because the film was weathering a storm of controversy, Time's Up, specifically the women of color in the organization, wanted to find a way to support Russell's accusers. We'd all gotten our coffees and pastries and were forming a big circle of foldout chairs in the middle of the conference room when the session's leader delivered a modest ask: "Let's go around the room and introduce ourselves. Please tell us your name, your occupation, and why you're here." Why are you here? Simple, right?

Women who were clearly braver than me in that moment talked about how they'd been hurt and how they'd overcome it. How they'd been put in horrible and dangerous situations by powerful people and somehow come out on the other side. How they wanted to make sure no one ever ended up in that same situation. Some of Russell's accusers were even there, once again living through their pain by rehashing their experiences. When it was my turn, the only thing I could say without crying was my name.

"I'm so sorry," I said through tears. "I'm not ready to tell my story yet. I will be at some point. Just not today." Nina was in that circle, and so was my friend Valerie Jarrett. There was support in that room. There was a community. But I still couldn't bring myself to say the thing aloud. I was so overcome with emotion that I barely heard another word for the next hour. But I left that morning determined to tell my story. This is it.

Bob Johnson and I were in a relationship that lasted many years, during which he regularly used his power as the head of

BET to control and manipulate me in the office and at home. It was a poisonous situation that slowly infected every aspect of my life. I didn't fully comprehend what I had suffered and the lasting damage it caused until the #MeToo and Time's Up movements shined a light on the hidden dark corners of the workplace. Being in those rooms, listening to those women tell stories that sounded so similar to my own? That's when I realized my experience was far from unique or rare. It started with a business trip.

For the first 10 years of our professional relationship, Bob and I were strictly colleagues. I considered him a mentor, a sponsor. Someone who never asked me if I could do something, he simply believed that I could. I admired him deeply. He was a visionary, and the lessons he taught me during my time at BET were invaluable. Without his unwavering confidence in my abilities, I might not have ever made the leap from lawyer to businesswoman. Bob Johnson taught me how to be a CEO. Before things changed between us, we'd been on countless trips together—for both business and pleasure. (BET rented a beach house in Delaware every summer for senior executives and their families, and he often invited execs and their spouses to various events.) On those occasions, he never did anything inappropriate or untoward.

The first time I felt the energy between us shift was during a trip to Los Angeles. I was staying at the Four Seasons Hotel in Beverly Hills, while Bob was spending his time at a friend's beach house in Malibu, a 50-minute drive west.

"Why don't you come over here tonight and I'll make dinner?" Bob asked at the end of a work call when just the two of us were on the line. "The view is amazing." I did a mental double take. The suggestion that we meet at a house and not a public restaurant? That he cook dinner for me? It seemed...intimate. We were friends who'd shared plenty of good wine and food together but there was a clear line. This felt different. Red flags were waving right in my face, but I swatted them away. This was Bob, after all. Bob was a friend, and we were both married.

Still, my gut told me to say no. But even that decision felt charged, as if I were accusing him of something by declining. Because there was a power differential between us, saying no to my boss was never just saying no. It meant something. It was certainly risky, and I didn't want to make this *a thing*. That's one of the many challenges of being a woman in the workplace; you always have a double consciousness. And being a Black female executive did not make it any easier. I still had to contend with the patriarchy and the boys' club; even if Bob made it a point to be egalitarian, egos were egos. He—and most of the men I'd worked with—had a big one. Learning how to dance around it was a skill as necessary as any. That was the additional burden of female leadership. You're forced to consider angles and consequences men wouldn't give a second thought. All the scenarios ran through my mind in the 10 seconds it took me to say, "Why don't we go to the Ivy instead?" I knew Bob would go for it because as much as he claimed to not be impressed with Hollywood types, dining at a well-known celebrity hot spot would pique his interest. "Great idea," he said. The subsequent dinner was like any other, no different from the hundreds of one-on-one sit-downs we'd had before. The two of us chatted as we would in the executive dining room back at BET HQ. No lines were crossed in that conversation. We talked about business, basketball, and our families. And yet the whole time there was a strange sinking feeling in the pit of my stomach as I recalled his first invitation. I labeled the entire incident with my "*Okay, that was weird*" sticker, hoping it would never happen again.

The invitation to dinner with just the two of us in a secluded location still bothered me, but I never said a word to Randy about it. He and I were having our own issues—struggling to make our high-flying careers and increasingly busy home life magically click together without giving an inch on either side. No one told me it would be this difficult, conquering the business world while building a family. My mother worked incredibly hard her entire life. She made juggling her 9-to-5, her husband, and her kids look, if not easy, at least doable. Plus, she did it with such elevated style and grace. But she wasn't a "career woman." Climbing up the corporate ladder meant sacrificing so much of what I was taught a "traditional" wife and mother was supposed to be—sitting in the front row at every school play, making small talk with your husband's colleagues at *his* networking events. My career and commitment to it were driving a wedge between Randy and me not because I couldn't be both a powerful executive *and* a loving supportive wife but because neither Randy nor I had sat still long enough to figure out how our grand ambitions fit into our marriage. We just assumed loving each other was enough to make it work. We assumed that two smart people could figure out the jigsaw puzzle of boardrooms, babies, and backyard barbecues. We assumed.

"*Money* magazine is on line one." My appointment as president and chief operating officer of BET in 1995 was starting to generate press. Having a woman lead a multimillion-dollar company that was going nowhere but up was a significant moment. The editor from *Money*, a national publication with major reach, wanted me for that month's anchoring story. A Black woman on the cover. My immediate reaction was joy. Then she laid out the concept.

"We're thinking boys' club chic. You'll be in a tailored pinstripe suit sitting at one of those old-school mahogany desks with your feet up and a fat cigar in one hand. Here's the headline: 'I don't need your money, honey.'"

"Oh no. No. I can't do that," I told the editor, who tried for the next 10 minutes to convince me that the cover would be tasteful. "It's a hair too far, don't you think? I'm grateful for the opportunity, but that concept is not going to work for me." What I didn't tell her was how devastating that image would have been to my marriage. I was the major breadwinner. I was the one gone most weeks to New York or Los Angeles. I was the one who took conference calls from the school parking lot. Randy and I were already on the rocks. Publicly announcing to the business community that I didn't need his money? I wouldn't do that to my husband. I couldn't disrespect him like that. The whole tone was wrong. My accomplishments didn't need to diminish Randy. The magazine didn't get that. How could it? All it saw was the provocative image of a female executive on the rise, not the Black woman married to a proud Black man. I couldn't be one and not the other. I deserved that cover, but Randy didn't deserve to have my paycheck rubbed in his face.

"Thank you, but no." In the end, they quoted me in the article about the power of investing as women, but I didn't get the cover. Navigating a modern marriage is a Herculean task for any ambitious couple with "we can have it all" fantasies dancing in their heads. But you can't succeed at partnership without approaching it with clear eyes and plenty of communication. That advice sounds obvious, but I can't tell you how many women CEOs I know who assumed that their marriages would work themselves out. We all know love doesn't pay bills. But you know what else it doesn't do? It doesn't allocate what percentage of your paycheck goes to said bills, divide up the house chores, or decide who'll pick up the kids when both parents are working well past 8 p.m. or who sits in the crowd clapping for whom. You have to see the value in showing up for each other. That's the part women have *been* doing for millennia. But men? He might seem perfectly happy with you flying off every Monday now, but don't take that initial bliss for granted. Marriage, any long-term relationship, is a marathon. Check in at every mile marker. Randy and I weren't doing that. He never knew about that *Money* magazine cover, but I did. It seemed as if the secrets between us were growing bigger and bigger.

"Where to this time?" Randy asked as he walked in on me packing a suitcase.

"Denver, I think," I replied with a heavy sigh, bracing myself for any negative feedback I might get from my husband. He missed me. The kids missed me. I missed them. We couldn't keep going like this. All the usual points. But this time my husband just said, "Okay," walked out of our bedroom, shut the door, and headed to his office.

Bob and I were in the elevator of our hotel when it happened. I was staying on 10, and he was, of course, on the penthouse floor. The two of us were chuckling about something I can't even remember now. But as always, the conversation was easy. It always was with Bob; even when he was being difficult, you still wanted to keep talking to him. The laughter died down, leaving an open space between us. He ran his finger down my arm in that slow, unmistakable way. "Debra," he said, making my name sound like a full sentence, a question. We kissed. The ding of the elevator forced my eyes open. *This can't happen*, I thought before breaking away and escaping down the hall to the safety of my room. He didn't call out to stop me or even mention it over breakfast the next morning. We sat across from each other eating our eggs and chatting about business as if nothing out of the ordinary had happened the night before. I had my good girl game face on—smiling and cordial. But inside I was reeling. What did it mean? Was it a fluke? Could we really just ignore it and move on? For his part, Bob was Bob. Even-keeled and always in control. His face gave nothing away. At the time, I didn't know how to feel. Guilt, excitement, anticipation, and dread were all mashed up together. We flew back to DC as if nothing had changed.

"How was it?" Randy asked as I walked in the house late.

"Fine," I said. Randy offered a half-hearted *umm-hmm* and then headed to bed.

For the next four or five months, I kept my distance from Bob. Whenever his assistant called mine to schedule a lunch or private meeting, my calendar blocks were increasingly unavailable. As COO and CEO, we obviously couldn't avoid each other entirely or for long. As his first point of contact for daily operations, Bob needed me in order to keep his finger on the pulse of the company. I tried to wiggle out of any commitments that weren't absolutely necessary, but those were few and far between. Bob noticed my absence, but instead of saying anything to me, he just made his power and influence felt. As CEO, he had control over whether I traveled with him. He also had a say in which hotels I stayed in. Slowly but surely the floors between our rooms started to condense. Soon we were saying good night and walking in opposite directions but on the very same floor. Then to doors right next to one another. What Bob was doing was obvious, but I never called him out on it. What could I say? It'd been months since our kiss. Months of me replaying that moment in my head. *Do I want to do this? Do I want to ruin my marriage? Should I just quit my job?*

Resisting the pull between the two of us was becoming next to impossible as we racked up more miles on the road together. It became not an if but a when. Then Bob finally made his chess move. After our meetings wrapped for the day, we usually met in the lobby of our hotel and ventured out to dinner from there. But on this particular evening, my room phone rang just as I was grabbing my jacket to head downstairs.

"Meet me in my room and we'll go down together," suggested Bob. *Here we go.* I knocked on his door, and Bob answered it shirtless. I smirked. Instead of taking the bait, I simply side-stepped him in the foyer and waited there. "Just a sec," he said before shrugging into his button-down and picking up his suit jacket. "Okay, let's go." *What's he doing?* I mean, I knew exactly what he was doing, but the dance, the chase, whatever this was, felt almost choreographed. I was falling into preordained steps.

By our next trip, sleeping together felt inevitable. I remember thinking, *I can't put this off any longer.* That isn't to say I lacked agency or that anything was forced upon me. I was a grown woman. I'd been married twice. I knew how to take control of and responsibility for my own actions. Still, something about this situation with Bob never felt like it was completely in my control. The line separating my life and BET had been so blurred for so long that being with Bob almost felt natural. Before Time's Up, I would have called our relationship completely consensual. Like I said, we were both grown. But, on reflection, there was obviously much more to it than that. Bob was my boss and had been for nearly a decade. The power he held over me wasn't something I could ignore. And listening to other women tell stories of how their own bosses followed Bob's playbook to a T—random candlelit dinners, meeting up in a hotel room, innocent run-ins that somehow turned intimate—I realized that the relationship Bob and I had for years was far from equal.

While I held on tight to the fact that Bob didn't make his move until after he'd offered me the COO position, I also knew that less than a year later we were "together." Whether or not I gave voice to this concern back then, there's no denying that turning Bob down would have affected my career. The man had just offered me the keys to the kingdom. If I rejected his advances, would I suffer for it? Would he retaliate against me at work? Would he fire me, demote me? Make managing the senior leadership team even harder than he already had? More importantly, I knew that my place in the corporate world, as a Black female COO, was a once-in-a-lifetime opportunity. Where else was I going to get the chance to lead a thriving company that was built for and run by Black people? Those were all questions I never asked myself aloud, but they were there in the back of my mind, influencing every choice I made when it came to Bob and me. I'd fought too long and too hard to earn the position I was in. Leaving the company was not an option for me.

The morning after, I secretly hoped that this was just a one-time thing. Following months of flirting and tension, we'd gotten it out of our systems, and now we would be able to both go back to our families. Then after the third and fourth times, I sunk deeper into insecurity. The fact that Bob offered me the COO position before we slept together began to mean less and less. *Was that all part of his plan? Did he offer me the job in the hopes of getting closer to me? Was my entire career just a cat-and-mouse game to him?* That was too outlandish, wasn't it? Not even Bob was that calculating. Right? Clearly, he knew I was capable of running the company. I went back and forth like that on repeat, making myself dizzy with worry and guilt. The moral ground was so muddy, the timeline of when we got involved so murky. I could never truly stand firm on one answer over the other.

In the beginning, our relationship was exclusively on the road. We only slept together when we were traveling for work. During those years, the affair felt like a thrilling escape, a second life I could slip into and out of. Bob was smooth. When the business of the day was done, he'd take me to the very best restaurants, where we'd sip expensive bottles of wine and dream up the future of BET on his personal dime. Despite all the real work we were doing, it felt like a vacation. Randy and I were increasingly unhappy. Being with Bob began as a fun distraction, but eventually it started to feel almost real, like something beyond hotel rendezvous. Something that could see the light of day and survive. Remember, Bob and I truly liked each other. We always had a connection, and now it seemed to be growing naturally into something more. Because in truth while the consequences of what we were doing were thousands of miles out of sight, our time together felt light and freeing. Eventually, though, the real world reared its head, and Randy and I decided to get divorced. I wasn't leaving my husband for Bob Johnson. While the affair most certainly didn't help the health of our relationship, our problems were our own. But the split did allow Bob and me to see each other more. Around the same time, Bob and his wife Sheila broke up. With both of us single by 2002, the relationship needed definition. In fact, our new bosses forced our hand.

In 2000, we sold BET to Viacom Inc. for $3 billion. Sumner Redstone, Viacom's longtime CEO, and his number two, Mel Karmazin, had approached Bob the year before, but he wasn't ready to sell the whole company, which had gone private again after several years as a publicly traded company. Bob asked Sumner if he'd be open to coming on as a partial owner. "I don't buy pieces. If I'm going to buy it, I want the whole thing," Sumner replied. After considering Viacom's proposal and going on a road show to solicit even more offers, Bob and John Malone decided that $3 billion was the magic number. If Viacom could do that *and* ensure that BET would continue to be run by Black executives, then he had a deal. "What do you think? Two Jewish guys are going to run BET," Mel joked before everyone shook hands and the deal was done. Bob and I both got five-year contracts. Being owned by a larger media conglomerate meant new rules, and one of them directly pertained to us. Viacom required all its executives to sign a new business conduct statement that clearly discouraged office romances. Once we'd settled into the larger corporate structure after a few years, it was clear (to me) that this policy affected us. According to our new bosses, you had to alert Human Resources if you were in a relationship with someone you reported to. Were Bob and I in a relationship? We were both unmarried and had been on and off for years. But I still hadn't told my family or my ex-husband about us. If Bob and I were really a thing, we'd have to alert the higher-ups.

"Have you seen this Viacom policy? Bob, you have to talk to the powers that be and tell them we're together."

"Oh, don't worry about that. It doesn't apply to us," he assured me.

"Did you forget I'm the lawyer? I know what this means. We're not exempt. Trust me. Just go tell them and see what they say." It took me a while to convince him that, as CEO and my boss, Bob should be the one to come clean about us to Viacom. That there was an us to come clean about. He reluctantly agreed. I never knew exactly how that conversation went or what exactly Bob said, but shortly thereafter, I officially was reporting to Tom Freston, who was running MTV and other Viacom cable networks. Now anytime Bob wanted to give me a raise or promotion, Tom had to approve it. It was a giant relief. That one organizational change lifted a weight off my chest I hadn't realized was there. I had assumed Viacom brass would want one of us to go. And I could hear my father's voice scolding me, "See, Debi. If anything goes wrong, you're the one who's going to suffer for it. Not him." It was the same thing he'd warned me about all those years earlier when Ernie and I moved in together at Harvard. He never wanted my career tied up with some man's. Yet here I was 20 years later in a situation that had the potential to blow up in my face. My dad would've been livid if he were still alive. I said a silent prayer when the decision was made about the change in my reporting. Having our relationship on the books at Viacom added legitimacy. Now no one could say we were sneaking around, despite the fact that we still hadn't come out as a couple to the rest of the world.

For a while, things were going well between us. But not for long. While disclosing our relationship to Viacom made it easier to eventually come out to our family and friends, it also meant we were now potentially a real couple. What did that mean for two people who worked together? The answer is murky. It meant that the lines dividing the office and "us" were always blurred. The personal and the professional were always intrinsically tied. If work was going well, then so went the relationship, but the opposite was also true. It was near impossible to separate Bob my boss from Bob my "boyfriend." I respected him and admired him, but was that love? Power dynamics aside, the muddling of those feelings is what makes office romances such dangerous territory. For a brief period, I thought we'd go the distance as a couple because work was going so well. As I became more comfortable in my role as COO, Bob was more than happy to teach me more of the business as the two of us zipped around the country and grew BET into a major media player. *We can do this*, I thought as the image of us as a power couple began to solidify—dinner with Bill and Hillary Clinton, posing on red carpets together. But Bob liked things the way they were—me as number two and him as number one. I'd spent more than enough time as COO by then, much longer than most would stay in that role before being appointed CEO. I knew the business, the players, the way forward. My training was beyond complete, but Bob still wanted to steer the ship. He didn't know how to give up control of BET, and his grip began to tighten at work and around my arm. The more comfortable I got with my own power and authority, the more Bob would act out to prove to me and everyone else who was really boss.

"Schedule a meeting with my buddy next week. He has this great idea for an animated series for next year."

"The programming calendar for next season is all set, Bob. We solidified that last week. This is a waste of time." The BET staff increasingly looked to me for answers. At times I felt like a pseudo-CEO and a big part of my job was explaining Bob's directives and getting him to change his mind when we were on the verge of a mutiny. Bob would often swoop in the last minute to make ridiculous asks or straight up reverse the decisions I made.

"It's not. He's good. I want everyone in on this—the programming teams, marketing—..." I rolled my eyes. This is what he did now. Coming in at the 11th hour to make changes that no one wanted and that I would just have to fix later. It made me look silly, but he was still my boss.

We were locking heads more often during the day, and whatever fight we had at work would carry over at home. Now that we had the freedom to be a real couple, I had to take a hard look at what being with Bob actually meant. Did we share the same values? Did we have the same vision for our individual futures outside work? After two divorces, I wanted a settled home life that included a loyal and supportive husband who understood that I was passionate about what I did. I wanted Quinn and Ava to thrive and feel like their home was a place of refuge. I wanted a soft landing, a partner who understood me and loved me unconditionally. Who knew that money didn't solve every problem. Who was empathetic and kind. Someone who truly loved people, not just what people could do for them. Was that Bob? Slowly but surely, I realized the answer was no. Bob was not that partner, and he couldn't give me the life I wanted when I took the time to truly dream up what that looked like. And if I ever wavered—reluctant to throw away years of companionship, if not true partnership—the continuing rumors about his affairs certainly helped turn that tide.

Once the two of us were sharing a bottle of wine after work when Bob's phone rang. It was 11 p.m. "I'll let the machine get it," he said. A young woman left a message about the two of them getting together the next day. I cocked an eyebrow. "I'm mentoring her," he told me with a straight face. There were always other women. I was never unique. Our relationship was a losing game. I wanted true monogamy, and Bob simply didn't believe in that. Without committing to a relationship and a willingness to be exclusive long term, this wasn't going to work. That's when I decided I wanted out. Bob didn't. And the tug-of-war between us would last for a couple more years. I'm not even sure Bob wanted to stay together. I'm more convinced he just didn't want leaving to be *my* decision, my choice. He wanted all the cards. That's when shit really hit the fan.

This is the thing about office romances, which have a wispy air of fairy tale about them that is neither accurate nor reliable. I want anyone, male or female, to really think hard before they enter a relationship with someone at work, especially your manager. The imbalance of power is impossible to leave at the office; it can easily boil over into every aspect of the relationship. If you want out—and let's be honest, most office romances end in tears—your former lover will rarely make leaving easy. Never assume that the two of you are going to walk hand in hand into the sunset without going through the fire first. Or that you'll still be holding hands instead of being at each other's throats. We all think we're different. Things can go well for a while, but what happens when things fall apart? Who will be forced to give up what? Despite the change in company structure per Viacom, I knew full well that if I wanted to break up with Bob, I would have to quit. How'd I know? The man told me as much.

My biggest fear was that our relationship would be a headline one day and that my dad's warning would come to bear. I would lose everything—my reputation, my job, my respect. While Bob would just be Bob. Folks would assume that my climb up the ladder had nothing to do with my talent. No one would understand what I was going through.

I stupidly thought that we could break up and still be friends. But Bob was clear that would never be the case.

"No, you and me? We are not friends. If you break up with me, you have to leave the company because I can't see you every day in the office if we're not together." He knew how heavy that threat was, especially when I became a single mother who was still recovering from the stress of a divorce.

The end was coming, and even though I was supposed to be in the driver's seat, Bob refused to take his hand off the wheel. So we started arguing about that. And by argue I don't mean heated discussions. We fought. Sometimes physically.

"Just name me president and CEO. You can still be chairman. I've been running this company for nearly 10 years. Why are we fighting about this now?" I'd plead.

"The time isn't right, Debra. I'm still around. People still need to see me as the face of BET."

"What are you talking about? Dragging this out is just making it harder on everyone."

"Everyone? Or you?"

I stormed out of his office seeing red and went home to catch the tail end of dinner with Ava. At around 11 p.m., my phone rang. I knew who it was before I said hello. Bob wanted to argue some more.

"Do you really think I'm trying to hurt you?"

"That's not what this is about, and you know it."

We went around and around like that for hours. I'd hang up, and he'd call back seconds later. He could keep this up all night. Eventually I had to walk from room to room turning off every phone in the house. I had no way to explain why this man was calling me at all hours. If I was home alone (Ava at her dad's, Quinn away at college), Bob wouldn't bother calling, he'd just show up to my house. He knew the security code to my gate. When I wouldn't open the front door, he'd go off, shouting and carrying on. If I let him inside, we'd just yell for hours on end. I wanted to find a resolution, a way out for both of us. But Bob just wanted to argue, keeping me up to the point of exhaustion. Sometimes it would become physical. I was trying to run a company and co-parent two teenagers with my ex while fighting with Bob for what felt like every waking minute. The stress threatened to pull me under. The worst thing was I had absolutely no one to confide in.

This became my new normal.

There were many, many breaking points, but the one that truly broke me happened during—what else?—another work trip. Bob and I were in Manhattan to go over the network's quarterly reports with Viacom's top brass, a task he did not enjoy. We fought the entire cab ride back to the hotel. I was done. I couldn't argue another second more. "We'll finish this upstairs," he hissed in my ear as the two of us walked into the lobby. "No, Bob. I can't. Just go to your room. We'll talk in the morning." I walked away as quickly as I could, my stilettos click-clacking against the stone floor. A warm bath was all I wanted. Solitude. Quiet. No more yelling. The tub was half full when I heard the automatic click of the door unlocking. It was Bob. The front desk had given him a key to my room with no questions asked. The hotel knew who we were and that we traveled together often. That was Bob's insidious power over me. There was no escape. He barged in. I tried to push him out. There was a tussle, and somehow I was able to slam the door in his face. He banged a fist against it and retreated for the night.

"Are you all right, Debi?" I was at an *Essence* magazine reception and had run into Terrie Williams, the former Hollywood power publicist who'd represented Miles Davis and Eddie Murphy. After a wildly successful run heading her own PR agency, Terrie had famously been forced to abandon the rat race after a bout of depression. She'd been preaching the gospel of mental health awareness ever since.

"I'm fine," I told her.

"You don't look well," Terrie told me with a concern that shook me to my core. I thought I'd been hiding it well. But this woman knew within moments that something wasn't right with me. My friend Yolanda, whom I'd known for more than a decade by then, echoed Terrie's concerns a short time later. "You need to talk to somebody," she told me. "I think all of this is becoming too much for you to handle." Not even Yolanda, whom I met through Bob in 1995 when she helped us plan our first *Walk of Fame* show, knew what was going on between Bob and me behind closed doors. But as a Washington insider who'd been involved in politics for decades, Yolanda knew all too well that relationships with bosses were not easy. The isolation is what really got me. It was already lonely at the top as one of the few Black female media executives; now add to that the fact that I was in a constant battle with the man I'd once considered my greatest ally and advocate. I felt trapped in a tiny cage with bars I'd helped build. There was no one to turn to. I couldn't confide in Randy because of the guilt. I couldn't tell my sister Gretta because I was too embarrassed. My big sister shouldn't have to bail me out again like she had when we were younger. I couldn't cry on my mother's shoulder because I felt too ashamed. Did I mention that she worked at BET? Bob had hired her as a part-time receptionist a few years before, and she treated that desk like her throne. Everyone in the office loved her. She was the company mom. How could I admit all this to her? How could I have gone from her pride and joy to this woman? Fear of judgment. Fear of ridicule. Fear kept me silent.

In 2004, an unauthorized biography called *The Billion Dollar BET* hit the shelves. The *Washington Post's* gossip column ran a quote from Bob's ex-wife, Sheila, who confirmed in the book what folks had been whispering about for years. "That affair with Debra just hurt me more than anything, because I knew her, and I couldn't believe she would do that. I find the whole thing tragic." It was tragic, but in more ways than she or anyone would ever know. I'd just landed back in DC from a much-needed vacation, and the first call I got was from Randy. He had seen the *Post* item and wanted to know if it was true that Bob and I were involved. I assured him it wasn't. This was May 2004 and Bob and I still weren't publicly dating—yet. But that August, Bob threw me a lavish 50th birthday party weekend in the Hamptons for 200 of his (and my) closest A-list friends. The over-the-top celebration was his way of making it clear to everyone that we were a couple.

We fought the whole time. I sat through his effusive toast to me with a smile on my face while feeling sick to my stomach. This wasn't what I wanted.

Hanging on to my sanity became harder. I wanted to end things but couldn't escape Bob's presence. He was everywhere. Like the time he showed up on Martha's Vineyard when I was there on vacation with Quinn and Ava. Bob and I had been fighting about something (we were always fighting about something), so I was looking forward to time away from DC and Bob. But less than a day into our trip, there he was knocking on the front door of our vacation home with a smile on his face as if he'd been invited. When you have a private plane and a lot of money, you can do whatever you want to do. The man always knew where I was. Just like that night at the hotel when he used a key I hadn't given him to get to me, my sense of privacy and security had vanished. Losing control over your own life feels like unraveling, the threads you've spent years weaving together picked apart one by one. All that's left is a pile of yarn on the floor.

Bob did such outlandish things it was impossible to recognize which way was up. Like the time he faked a terminal illness to cover up one of our arguments. Staying on as COO under his thumb was pressing down on my soul so much I had very little left for myself. "I'm done," I said late one night during one of our marathon phone sessions.

"Well, if you're breaking up with me, then you have to quit, and you have to announce it to the senior team."

"All right, I'll do it," I said, too exhausted to keep going.

"Tomorrow."

"What?"

"I'm going to call an emergency conference call tomorrow morning, and you do it then so we can get this over with."

"Okay," I said before hanging up.

Early the next morning, Bob insisted that I drive to his house to sit next to him on the conference call to announce my resignation. It made zero sense. But I was so over him by then it didn't matter. I'd do whatever needed to be done to get this man out of my life for good. When I arrived at his mansion in Forest Hills, Bob was all contrition, all apologies, all sweet nothings. We made up. Like we usually did.

Our toxic pattern had been played and replayed so many times I was begging for someone to cancel us. Whenever Bob would get mad at me—over some decision I made at work or something I said in our private time after hours—the first thing he'd say was, "I'm going to call Michele and tell her you can't use the plane." That was his billy club, leaving me stranded on a business trip, scrambling to find my own way to a scheduled investment meeting or, worse, back home to Washington. He used his power to punish me like I was a child. He knew it was about more than flying private. It was about embarrassing me, disrupting my schedule as a senior executive, and proving that in the end, Bob had all the control. Once we got into an argument at the exclusive CEO conference in Sun Valley, Idaho, and I remember being so grateful we'd made up before the end of the conference because otherwise I'd have to figure out how to get home on my own.

When we made up that morning at his home, I was relieved because it meant that I could unclench—at least until our next inevitable blowup. But, in this case, there was a problem—the emergency senior staff conference call that Bob had scheduled was still on the books. Bob didn't want to raise concerns by canceling it, so the meeting went ahead.

"What's the emergency?" asked one of the executives once everyone was on the call.

Bob waited a beat and then proceeded to deliver insane three words:

"I have cancer," he said into the speaker, not even bothering to glance my way. There were audible gasps and *oh nos*. "Don't worry, the prognosis is good, and I'll be okay. I just wanted to let you all know first." Robert L. Johnson did not have cancer then. But he told a gathering of the senior executives at the billion-dollar company he ran that he did in order to save face for calling an emergency meeting just to threaten me. This was beyond.

"Well, that was…an odd choice," I told him. "They're going to find out the truth eventually." He assured me that they wouldn't. I never saw Bob so plainly as I did in that moment. The man would do anything—including tell a bald-faced lie about having cancer—to inflict his authority. His power was like a bullet, and I was done being target practice.

In the end, my exit strategy was deceptively simple: Just hold on. My goal was to hang on for the last 18 months remaining on Bob's contract with Viacom. He'd leave, I'd be named CEO, and all the pain would be worth it. The "relationship" had been effectively over for months by that time. All we did when we were together was argue. There was no love between us then if there ever was to begin with. But my resolve constantly wavered. "I can't do this anymore," I told my friend Thomas. "I have to get out of here before I go crazy." Like everyone else, he had no idea what was really going on, but his words helped guide me back to my North Star. "You're only a year and a half away," he replied. "You can make it 18 months."

I could make it 18 months. And when I thought I couldn't stay a minute longer, there were 12 months left and then only six and two months. Down the clock went until Bob was finally on his way out the door. I had been at the company for almost two decades. Was Bob going to write my story and decide how it ended? Or would I take what was mine? I wanted to be CEO. I deserved to be CEO. And I could not give Bob the satisfaction of running me off. Those were the longest 18 months of my life. It got rough. As we got closer to the handoff, Bob grew more desperate to prove he was still in charge while I grew more bold, unafraid to speak my mind and openly contradict the boss's random edicts. "No, we're not doing that," I'd say during a programming meeting in response to one of Bob's 11th-hour notes, and that was that. No explanation needed. Let's move on to the next item on the agenda, please. I don't think Bob wanted me to fail outright. I just don't think he knew how to let me succeed without him. The sea swells of his moods were giant, but I hung on for dear life.

In June 2005, Bob released this statement to the press: "I could not have chosen a better chief executive and outstanding leader to succeed me at BET than Debra Lee, and that's what makes this announcement so important to me and positive for BET's future. Few executives in this industry have exhibited the ability to manage a unique growth company and shown the commitment to building a successful brand the way Debra has in her 19 years at BET. She mastered the cable programming industry long ago and has a strong executive team in place to support her as she leads BET within the Viacom family."

The announcement was bittersweet and more than a little baffling. All anyone would conclude from reading it was that Bob and I had a good working relationship based on mutual respect. It was a joke. If I could rip it up and throw it in the trash, I would have. Instead, I filed it away with the growing pile of disrespect and indignities Bob had given me over the previous decade and got to work. I had something for him. A final F you.

Will Smith and Jada Pinkett Smith were hosting the BET Awards later that month. The show was in its fifth year and had been crushing the ratings since its premiere. With the CEO announcement in the can, Bob decided that the awards show broadcast would be his official swan song.

"I want you to give this speech," he told me, handing me a page of paragraphs about how great he was. I read it and gave him a tight smile. "Sure, Bob."

The night of the show I walked onto that stage with Bob trailing beside me. I wore a saucy black evening gown paired with dangling diamond earrings. I stepped up to the mic and looked out on the crowd at the Kodak Theatre in Los Angeles, which was packed with industry heavyweights like Halle Berry, Mariah Carey, Magic Johnson, Nelly, Stevie Wonder, Destiny's Child—heck, even Tom Cruise was there to present an award. These people didn't know what it took to get me to that mic. What they saw was a woman about to take the throne. They saw a woman in charge, so I decided to see that too.

"Good evening. First, I want to thank Viacom and BET for the incredible opportunity to lead this amazing company. Now, of course, Bob had a speech prepared for me," I said, not looking to the man standing right there on my left. "But you know what? I'm taking over, and Bob Johnson can't tell me what to say."

CHAPTER NINE

LEADING LIKE A WOMAN

"Debra," she said in a nervous tremble that I recognized in my own voice more times than I cared to count, "can we talk?" asked one of my female executives, already heading to a precious quiet corner of the Shrine Auditorium. "Now?" I asked, doing a halfway spin to take in the theater, which was buzzing with organized chaos as the network prepared for the ninth annual BET Awards airing live in 24 hours. We were in crisis mode, and she knew it. Michael Jackson, the icon whose songs provided the soundtrack for all our lives, had died suddenly the day before. Michael, *our* Michael. There was no question that the entire show would be dedicated to the King of Pop, which meant we had to start from scratch with less than 24 hours to get it right. "This can't wait," she said.

The two of us huddled together in a vacuum of silence,

and I turned to my senior executive, a talented young woman I'd worked with for years, to find out what was so important. "What's going on?"

"If Chris goes on that stage—if *you* let him perform—I'm going to quit," she said matter-of-factly. That questioning tremor in her voice was completely gone now. There was zero uncertainty as she looked me directly in the eyes to deliver her ultimatum. If I allowed Chris Brown—the pop singer who months before had admitted to physically assaulting his then-girlfriend Rihanna—to pay tribute to his hero, Michael Jackson, then one of the few women on my team would quit. She then confided in me that she was a survivor of domestic assault and there was no way she could continue working for a company that would give Chris Brown the honor of memorializing Michael Jackson.

For a split second, an annoying question popped into my head: *What would Bob do?* But I banished that thought just as quickly. I was CEO—had been for nearly four years. This was my company now. My seat was at the head of the table. I'd sacrificed more than any executive should to get here. So there was no way I was going to hand back control (even just a thought) to any of the men I had to wrestle it from in the first place.

I was Debra Lee. What did it mean to be me? To lead as me? I had to manage differently. If all I'm going to do is follow the senior male executive playbook, then what was the point? What was I doing in the top spot if, in the end, I was just a carbon copy of the men who'd come before me? I had to bring my whole self to the position and lead like me, not anyone else.

The problem is that exactly *how* to lead is not a lesson most managers receive before being put in charge. It happens on the fly; you figure it out as a you go. Mistakes are inevitable. You will fail miserably—in front of people. But good leaders are honest with themselves. They figure out what went wrong and they adjust immediately; they course correct.

"Debra?" she asked, wanting my answer right then and there.

"Thank you. I can't imagine how hard it was to share that with me. Whatever decision you make, I support you fully, you know that. But *this* decision? As CEO I have to consider every possible angle. But know I won't make it lightly." That wasn't the answer she wanted. But it was what I had to give, and I hoped it would be enough until I finally figured things out.

Because I was a woman, not only did I see both sides of the debate very clearly, but I also weighed them differently. When my executive gave me that ultimatum, the seriousness of the situation set in on not just a branding level but a personal one. I always knew the images we put out into the world meant something to the viewers at home, but they meant something to my staff on the other side of the screen too. Being a female CEO gave me a different outlook on what leadership was and how my core values played into my management decisions. Basically, it was never just business—not for a Black woman leading the top Black cable network in the industry. All eyes were on us, on me. So what did I stand for? And by extension, what did I want BET to stand for?

We were in an impossible situation. Michael was gone. Chris Brown wanted to go onstage. And BET's core values as a company and my success as a leader were being called to the mat. Our identity was being tested that weekend. Coming out on the other side as a stronger brand and team would solidify the work I'd been doing for the past several years. BET, the brand, had to stand for something.

My transition from COO to CEO was a lesson in forced patience. It took me six years to build my own executive team at BET. That is unheard of. It's unacceptable. As the chief operating officer of a billion-dollar business, I should have been surrounded by loyal and dedicated employees ready to roll up their sleeves and do the work alongside me once I made the leap to CEO. That wasn't what happened. After I became COO, some folks started cutting up on day one. One executive would strut into the executive conference room about 10 minutes late with a copy of the *Washington Post* in hand, sit down with a sigh, and then dramatically open up his broadsheet and start reading the day's news while the meeting was going on. Another started showing up to meetings in sunglasses. While this ridiculously immature pissing contest was going on, I was trying to run a company. Over time I'd learned that my leadership style was less hammer and more glue. Consensus and connection were the building blocks that allowed a company to move in the direction of a shared vision. But that hadn't been Bob's way, so my softer touch as a leader was immediately mistaken for weakness. The thing was, as COO I needed these executives. Programming and advertising were still new to me, so I depended on the heads of those departments.

"Can I see what we have coming up for next year?" I asked the programming head.

"Sure," he'd say and then never follow up. I'd ask for a list of viewership reports and never receive them. I'd call a meeting to go over advertising rates, and no one in the room would be prepared with the numbers. I was chasing my tail, managing hundreds of people, the top tier of whom did not want to see me win. The programming head even once made a presentation to the executive team, with me and Bob in the room, that was entitled "Why BET Sucks." The testosterone in the executive conference room was suffocating. I hated walking into that swamp, and I was stuck with it for years as COO because as a new manager you need a team with institutional knowledge. A mass exodus would have made things even worse. But I kept that famous Maya Angelou line top of mind: "When people show you who they are, believe them." When I eventually became CEO, when the decisions were mine and mine alone, I knew exactly who had to go. Anyone who was actively undermining me or just shirking their responsibilities was out. I had to get comfortable with uncomfortable conversations.

Management would be easy except for the people. That became one of my favorite sayings. Hiring and firing are an essential part of leadership. You have to enjoy hiring, and you have to learn to suffer through firing. It took me a while to look at someone in the face and say, "You are not doing a good job." My approach was always to give my staff a chance to improve before severing ties. This was a relationship, after all. As a leader, your job is to support your team as best you can in order for them to do their best work. At one point, I swear there were more executive coaches walking our halls than actual executives. That was the kind of leader I wanted to be, someone who gave opportunities instead of just snatching them away without warning. This was a business, but it was also BET. We were more than a collection of employees and managers; we were a community who supported our own—or at least we should have been. A handful of executives turned their departments around and began performing better; others refused the help. They had to go. A team is a living thing; it grows and grows stagnant. A manager's job is to consistently water and prune.

"Look, this is obviously not working out for you or the company. I think it is best you resign or I'm going to have to let you go." I'd hired McKinsey, the top-notch consulting firm, to come in and help me be the bad guy. What they say is true—consultants give you a reason to do what you wanted to do in the first place. Many COOs would start their first meeting pointing at people and telling them to pack their bags: "You four are gone." They have a vision for the company, and they execute immediately. McKinsey gave me the confidence and the support to do what I wanted to do. That started the transition in the office. But the biggest transformation was mental.

As COO, I had to learn how to take risks because that's not something they teach you in law school. Attorneys are supposed to be risk averse. All we see are the pitfalls, never the prize on the other side should you survive the leap. One thing about Bob: He was a lightning-fast decision maker. He saw something he wanted, and he took it—good or bad. I learned from him how to trust my gut when it came to business decisions. He'd see an idea and say, "BET should do that." That's what led us to the restaurants, clothing line, clubs, and casinos. At one point, he even decided that BET should start its own online platform. "I'm going to call Bill Gates!" If a business failed, it was just a blip. Learn and move on. Make the leap without worrying about whether the parachute might open. That's what led me to cancel *Uncut*.

I was slightly buzzed and more than a little bold at Bob's big goodbye party at the Four Seasons Hotel in Los Angeles during the fifth annual BET Awards weekend. More than a hundred A-listers were there to toast Bob and congratulate me as the new CEO. The champagne was flowing freely, and I was feeling, well, free. An unseen hand passed me another flute of bubbly when it was my turn to say a little something about Robert L. Johnson. I stood in front of the crowd and said what was on my mind because there was nothing anyone could do about it. What might have felt like a risk to the Debra of 19 years before was really a reinvention.

"Well, Bob sure does love a party, doesn't he?" I began before giving my former boss a light roasting in front of the crowd of Hollywood and music industry insiders. Since arriving to the party, I'd been thinking about all that we had gone through, all that I'd survived. But the moment still felt like a triumph. He was leaving, and I was taking the stage. Before I sat down, I made one last announcement: "Oh and I'm canceling *Uncut*."

"You're doing what? Ms. Lee, no!" That was Nelly yelling from the audience. There were other murmurs too. I think I heard Ludacris.

"Sure am," I said matter-of-factly before taking my seat at the main table. Funny thing is I had never even seen *Uncut*, the raunchy late-night video program the network got so much flak for. I knew it had to go. The program didn't fit with my new vision for BET that was slowly crystallizing in my head. That announcement, the night of Bob's glitzy goodbye, was my way of saying, "There's a new sheriff in town." Whatever nice and cozy relationship some of the bigwigs in the room thought they had with Bob would not translate over to my BET. I had a strategy to improve the network to compete with MTV and VH1. I wanted to win, not just "paint it Black," as Bob used to say. I'd spent so many years losing parts of myself to him while struggling to manage a company he wouldn't give up that as soon as I could take control, I did.

So, by the time Bob left for good six months later, we were well prepared. This was a long time coming. After a small gathering on the sixth floor, Bob said a few words, and the entire team walked with him outside into the cold January morning. He turned to wave, and dozens of balloons were sent up into the air. I walked back into the office and let go a decade of stress in one deep, heavy sigh. *Okay, he's gone. My turn now.*

Being the boss meant more than just redecorating Bob's CEO suite, which included an office, a conference room, and a private dining room; it meant that I had to make BET my own. I called in some help.

Ratings never mattered to Bob, and he was partially right. Because BET was the only game in town for years, the channel didn't have to fight for Black viewers. But times had changed. Now there were other Black networks like TV One, and the white networks had finally woken up to the fact that Black people enjoyed seeing themselves on the small screen. The day TV One, a network owned in part by radio titan Cathy Hughes, launched, I called Mel Karmazin, the COO of Viacom, and said, "BET might have some legit competition now." His advice was optimistic, "Don't worry, Debra. Competition makes the leader stronger." He was absolutely right. We couldn't call ourselves winners until we had someone to beat. And beat them we did. Competition marked the beginning of the strongest ratings in BET's history. But to keep our loyal viewers, we needed to to stand for something. Being Black was no longer a brand. What made BET different than VH1?

A white guy named Stan Slap helped us figure it out.

I'd heard Stan speak at an annual conference that Bill Gates hosted for CEOs. He was a tall man with a mop of jet-black hair streaked on the sides with gray. He wore thick black glasses and a suit but no tie as he paced the stage like a cool college professor and explained to a room full of corporate leaders how to build their brands. BET needed this guy. Before my plane touched down in Washington, the network had hired the Slap Company to help us define who we were and plant our own flag. I knew BET was different. We cared about viewers. We didn't just see them as dollar signs. Our ratings were good, but I wanted every Black household in the country to have their TV tuned to BET the moment they woke up in the morning.

"We need help," I told Stan when he arrived in DC for our first day of meetings.

"This is going to be hell," he said. "But at the end of it, I'll hand you the keys to heaven. I promise." At first, none of the senior executives saw the point of spending days away from their own teams theorizing about what BET meant to them and how the network impacted the world. "It's mandatory," I told my latest programming head, "and we're going to be happy about it." On top of leading hours-long sessions with the top-level team, Stan and his company spent months interviewing all our critics and our stakeholders—advertisers, cable operators, viewers, politicians. *What do you think of BET?* he'd ask. *How has the network made your life better—or worse?* The answers surprised us. "All they air is music videos. Boring." "They don't respect women." "Their shows are so low budget." "My great-auntie watches it, but I don't." It was heartbreaking. Stan made us take a hard look in the mirror and face up to the fact that the company had gotten lazy.

Bob's philosophy of not reinventing the wheel had kept our employees from truly investing in their own work. There was even a time when folks were too embarrassed to tell their families that they worked for BET, the channel that did nothing more than air videos of fully clothed rappers and scantily clad women all day.

"What do we do? How do we turn this around?" I asked during Stan's presentation in DC.

"Tell me what your values are. When you walk through the

lobby doors every morning, you should feel good. You should feel like you're living your values," he said.

The dozen of us in the room, the leaders of the company, came up with 10 buzzwords and then narrowed them down to three: family, community, and uplift. Then he made us talk about what the company should stand for. The team came up with three more words: respect, reflect, and elevate. That's how we wanted to treat our audience. That's what made us different from the other networks.

After 18 months of soul searching, our marching orders were clear: If anything we did didn't meet two of our brand values, then we didn't do it, period. That went for programming, advertising, business partnerships, community events—all of it. Going forward, BET would be a company that respected, reflected, and elevated its audience.

Which leads us back to Chris Brown.

When we'd launched the BET Awards in 2001, the ceremony was one in a long list of live awards shows. There were the Grammys plus the Video Music Awards, the American Music Awards, the Billboard Awards, and the Country Music Awards. We weren't even the only show centered on Black artists. The Soul Train Music Awards had been going strong since the late 1980s, and the NAACP's Image Awards had been around even longer. But BET had a special sauce. We were younger, fresher, tapped into the pulse of what was happening. Despite not bringing in earth-shattering ratings, we were still one of the biggest nights in music. Comedian and actor Jamie Foxx was hosting that year. New Edition was reuniting onstage. And yes, even Bobby Brown was supposed to show up. Beyoncé and her boyfriend Jay-Z were performing. Our show, just days away, would be the first official memorial to Michael Jackson. We had to get it right.

Stephen Hill, my head of programming specials, was a massive MJ fan. Massive. The man had every concert T-shirt from all of Michael's major tours. Stephen was more determined than anyone to do Michael and the entire Jackson family proud. "We're going to revise the whole show," he said during the crisis meeting. "Okay," I said. "Let's get to work." We brainstormed a set list of Michael's greatest hits and talked about which artist would perform them. We ripped up Jamie's opening skit and started from scratch. We knew the comedian could sing but "Can he dance?" someone asked. He ended up learning the moves to "Beat It." That conference room was a tornado of ideas and grief and celebration. Hours later the team emerged with a clear mission. Talent managers, choreographers, costume designers, and publicists needed to be called. New songs had to be learned and rehearsed; set design was going to change. It was a gigantic undertaking. But I was confident we were on the right track. This was Thursday, and the live show was Sunday. But I had full confidence that my team would make it happen. Then tech rehearsal happened.

T-minus two days until the show I was in the middle of a production meeting at the Shrine, the same place where in 1984 Michael Jackson's hair caught on fire while filming a Pepsi commercial for the Super Bowl. The historic theater is a colossal space, and yet it felt nearly claustrophobic that day as so much activity was swirling over every inch of the space. While trying to listen to a stage manager go through new marks, I heard an argument turn up a few rows behind me. Heated debates are not uncommon during stressful live events, but this one sounded different. Voices weren't just raised; they were at a fever pitch.

"No, no, no. There's no way we can do this."

"It's done!"

"He does not deserve to be on that stage right now."

"Well, tell that to Stephen because it's happening!"

Here's what I'd gleaned once I'd gotten to the bottom of things: In the 24 hours since our meeting the day before, Stephen, the super-duper Michael Jackson fan, had unilaterally decided that Chris Brown would be the artist to perform the ceremony's formal tribute to the King of Pop. "Chris is the only one who can do it," Stephen explained to me. "He loves Michael. And Michael loved him." But not everyone on the production team felt the same way. Earlier that same week, in a Los Angeles courtroom, Chris had pleaded guilty to assaulting Rihanna. That was on a Monday. Michael died on Thursday. And here we were on Saturday debating whether the baby-faced prince of R&B could pay tribute to the undisputed King of Pop. It was dizzying. The shock and betrayal still fresh. Sure, Chris loved MJ (we *all* did), but did that mean we should let him take over the biggest stage on the biggest night of the year to pay tribute to the biggest star? Stephen's vote was yes. The noes were picking up plenty of steam.

"What about our new brand?" one executive asked. "Respect, reflect, elevate? Does Chris represent any of those ideals right now? The audience won't like this."

We had a problem on our hands. Actually, *I* had a problem. Because after the credits rolled, the decision was mine to make. The negative headlines the next day would mention my name, no one else's. And that's when one of my executives pulled me aside to deliver an ultimatum: "If Chris goes on that stage, I'm going to quit."

In moments like this, as you walk away, time speeds up and slows down. You can see the tiniest movement traveling through the air and all the thousands of ripples and reactions your actions might cause. All while the clock is loudly ticking down to the moment of truth: your final decision. I still wasn't sure what the right move was. But what I knew above all else was that this was an opportunity to truly lead. Yes, we were grieving. We were fighting. None of us had really slept in the last 24 hours. But if I could steer the ship through a storm like this, then the team I'd been gradually pulling together since taking over as CEO would be unsinkable.

Back at the Shrine Auditorium, the team was still running through all the possible best- and worst-case scenarios when Stephen interrupted. "I just got off the phone with the label," he said, "and they say Chris is committed."

"Committed?" I did a double take. Yeah, no. Nothing had been written in stone, and no contracts had been signed. I put my lawyer hat on—the one Bob used to always tell me to take off once I became COO—and let Stephen know that there was no "commitment" until I said so.

The head of Chris's label, RCA/Jive, was a man named Barry Weiss. I knew Barry personally. Our sons had a mutual friend. But this call skipped the small talk and we got right down to business.

"Stephen asked us," Barry told me. "You guys can't go back on your word."

Oh, how I just loved when men told me what I could and couldn't do as the CEO of my own company. After nearly two decades at BET, I still had to remind people of my title and what that entailed. I always wondered if it was because I was Black or a woman or both. Of course, it was all of those things. Despite my having earned the right to my own mind, too often men still demanded I explain my decisions. But it was a speech I knew all too well. My voice was done shaking though. As a female leader, you're never done proving yourself in a male-dominated business, especially in the male-dominated entertainment industry. But that doesn't mean you should ever feel the need to explain yourself or your power to anyone. You've earned it—most likely by doing more for less for far too long. Your power is yours to wield as you see fit, and you don't have to apologize for it.

"I'm the head of the network, so whatever Stephen told you is not going to tie my hands. You'll have my answer tomorrow." I didn't apologize or hedge. This was my choice, and I was making it without pretense. Even with the unwavering knowledge that I was the decider—God, that sounds so silly—I wasn't the type of leader who came to her decisions lightly or alone. Ever the lawyer, facts, research, data points, and differing opinions helped reassure me. Yes, I had the power to put Chris on that stage or veto the whole thing. But first I wanted to know what others thought. The thing about business decisions is that they are not scientific. You can have the very best research at your fingertips—ratings, focus groups—but in the end, most conclusions come down to your gut instincts. Data is instructive, but it isn't the end all be all. Use it sparingly and trust yourself always. As far as Chris went, I was already leaning heavily toward my decision but wanted some backup in the way of group consensus. Be careful what you ask for.

The floodgates opened wide.

The first voicemail I got was from Chris's mother, Joyce. A mama bear through and through, she respectfully went to bat for her son. Joyce, herself a survivor of domestic violence, didn't excuse what Chris had done. He was wrong—and he'd owned up to it. Shouldn't he be allowed onstage? I still didn't know the answer to that, but I knew someone who might: the Black Godfather.

"Clarence, it's Debra." I'd solicited the advice of Clarence Avant, the man who for decades had been behind every major deal signed by every major Black artist in the music industry.

Clarence had seen it all and he knew everybody. If anyone could give me some perspective, it was him. As an added bonus he was from my hometown of Greensboro, North Carolina, or at least a small town nearby. So we had a close relationship. And he always answered the phone, ready and happy to offer up his wisdom to those who needed it. That was invaluable for a woman like me navigating an industry like ours where the movers and shakers and gatekeepers were often an old boys' club.

"We have this new brand identity and—"

"Forgive him," said Clarence. "Let him perform. Part of your brand is family, and Chris could be anybody's brother. Everyone deserves a second chance, Debra. We're all in this together, right? Chris is family too, isn't he?" Great, just what I needed—more questions. Yes, Chris was family. I'd been following the R&B singer since he was a kid. BET was one of the first networks to air the thumping dance video for his debut single "Run It!" But Rihanna was family too, wasn't she? It was interesting that so far no one questioned whether we'd be hurting her (or alienating her team) by letting her abuser onstage.

To clear my head, I took a walk down Santa Monica Boulevard near the Four Seasons Hotel where everyone in town for the show was staying. The white noise of traffic, tourists, and the rustling trees lining the thoroughfare helped center my mind. Then my cell phone rang with a number I didn't recognize. I decided what the heck and picked up. Maybe it was God calling to tell me what to do.

"Ms. Lee? This is Tito. Tito Jackson."

"Oh, hi."

"I just want you to know that the family is in support of Chris Brown."

"Really?"

"Yeah, we really want him to perform," said Tito, one of Michael's older brothers and one-fifth of the famous Jackson 5.

"Well, Tito," I said, still not able to comprehend that Tito Jackson, the guy I watched play the guitar with his brothers on *The Ed Sullivan Show*, had somehow gotten my personal cell number and was delivering a message from "the family." "Thank you for letting me know."

I headed back to the hotel no more certain than when I'd left. And who should I see pulling up to the Four Seasons in a Rolls-Royce convertible? Queen Latifah. I practically yelped. This was perfect. We'd given her a "Best Actress" nod the year before. As a veteran of the entertainment business and a rap pioneer who wasn't afraid to call out misogyny in hip-hop, Latifah was the perfect person for my informal poll. I could almost cry. Was there anyone else in the country who would understand the ins and outs of this situation better than her? I doubted it. *This was going to be good*, I thought as I ran down the situation to get Latifah's big take.

"Yeah, that's a tough one," she said. And left it at that.

Okay, that was a sign. The time for talking it out was over. With hours left to make the call, I put my big girl pants on and instead looked inward. There was so much pressure on me to let Chris perform. But the night belonged to MJ. If Chris went on that stage, then the next day's headlines would be all about him—positive or negative. I wanted the story to be about Michael Jackson and how BET, the first network by and for Black people, was also the first to pay its respects to the King of Pop. I couldn't let Chris Brown overshadow the whole thing or, worse, somehow mar Michael's legacy. That was my business mind talking, and it made sense. Equally important was my heart, and it was aching for Rihanna. The network had to support her as well. While she didn't ask for it specifically, I would stand behind her and not put a spotlight on her abuser just days after the two had been in court together. I couldn't do that. I wouldn't. The same went for my executive who'd threatened to quit and my daughter and all the young women who'd be watching from home.

That meant I had one final call to make that day before heading into meeting after meeting to smooth out all the major changes to the live show on Sunday.

"Barry, I can't do it. Chris won't be onstage tomorrow," I told his label head.

"I'm disappointed." That was fine. A little (or a lot of) disappointment never killed anybody. Leaders have to be okay with the fact that everyone won't get what they want. It's an oldie but a goodie—you can't please all of the people all of the time. But here's the remix: If you can please the right people—not the most powerful or most popular—then you're golden.

I hung up with Barry and took a minute to bask in the moment. I'd done it. It wasn't easy or even straightforward, but a choice was made, and I stood by it with zero regrets. Then I turned my phone off.

The show was spectacular. It was four hours of praise and worship. New Edition (yep, Bobby showed) opened the ceremony with a medley of Jackson 5 hits, including "ABC" and "The Love You Save." Joe Jackson was in the front row. Our host, Jamie, danced onto the stage in Michael's iconic red-leather jacket from "Beat It" and told the grieving crowd that we didn't "need to be sad"—Michael was ours, and we were sharing him with the world. "When somebody dies," preached Jamie, "we celebrate." While accepting her award for Best Female R&B Artist, Beyoncé thanked Michael Jackson for being her "hero." Alicia Keys said she felt Michael's spirit in the room. Even Janet Jackson, so fresh in her pain, came to the stage to remind us all that "To you, Michael is an icon. To us, Michael is family." Everyone who loved him and his music needed that night.

The next day I ran into Reverend Al Sharpton at the Four Seasons. "Congratulations on a great show, Debra," he said as we both stood in the hotel's lobby. I appreciated Al's compliment, but what he said next really warmed my heart and reinforced my decision about Chris performing onstage. "The Jackson family was very happy with the tribute to Michael," Al added. I guess Tito was not representing the entire family after all.

The next week Clarence Avant called (I had to turn my phone back on) to congratulate me too. "Oh, you made the right decision, Debra."

"You told me to let him onstage!"

"Well," said Clarence, "that was before I talked to my wife, Jackie!"

CHAPTER TEN

THE PASSION PHASE

It was the call from Oprah that did it. That's when I knew we were winning.

"Debra, you know I never thought we had a personal issue, but my people are telling me there's a problem," said Oprah, *the* Oprah Winfrey, to me during a one-on-one I'll never forget.

"Oprah, I have no idea what you're talking about," I countered. Now that wasn't *entirely* true. I had an inkling but wanted to see where this would go because I knew where it had started.

After the Chris Brown situation, word spread fast that Ms. Lee did not play. BET was not doing business as usual. My tastes became the network's. I wanted our audience to see that there was a range of possibilities for them. To "elevate" we began hosting *BET Honors* and *Black Girls Rock*, along with the Hip Hop Awards. And I sat in the front rows of the Hip Hop Awards every year because I wanted to remind the men in the auditorium, onstage, and watching from home that a woman was running the network. We started getting stricter when it came to standards and practices. Backup dancers during live performances needed to be PG-13 approved. All curse words would be bleeped. LeToya Luckett found me backstage at an awards show once and said, "Ms. Lee, I have a new video, and I think you're going to like it." I raised an eyebrow.

"It's very tasteful," she said. They were getting it. Well, some of them were.

When Stephen Hill brought me Kanye West's "Flashing Lights" video for approval, my first reaction was an immediate no. This wasn't about the music. It was about the images and the message they conveyed to an audience we'd finally convinced to trust us again. I couldn't see past the half-dressed video model strutting up a dark road on her way to stabbing Kanye, who was tied up in the trunk of her car. Was this hitting even one of our brand standards?

"I'm not putting that on BET. That has no redeeming social value," I told Stephen.

"You have to look past what's there, Debra. Kanye's a genius!" Stephen shot back, "And if we don't air this, you know he's going to call you."

"Let him," I said.

"MTV is airing this right now. It's hot."

"I don't care what MTV is doing," I told Stephen and the rest of the team, who stood there looking at me as if I said the Earth was flat. Everyone was freaking out, terrified that Kanye West would call BET and demand that we air a three-minute video that looked like an ad for Victoria's Secret. News flash, Kanye did not call me and complain.

If I had to be the only adult in the room, then so be it. My thumbs-down was legend. Aretha had taught me well all those years ago.

We had the same discussion about Rihanna's video for "Bitch Better Have My Money," a seven-minute-long revenge fantasy based on the singer's real-life drama with the accountant whose alleged bad advice cost her millions. The final frame featured Rihanna smoking a cigarette while lounging naked save for a few dollar bills stuck to her bloodied body. As much as I respected Rihanna and loved her music, I could not allow the video as it was even if it was made by a female artist. "Yeah, no," I told Stephen, who already knew what my answer would be. Black was no longer our sole branding strategy. We served a specific Black audience in a specific way. We didn't have to play every music video by every Black artist just because they wanted us to. We were not the only game in town, and we had our own standards. Word got out that we were being tougher. BET was no longer beholden to the music industry and music videos for content. Also, I hadn't forgotten how silent most of those same artists were when protestors were gathered outside my home demanding that BET stop showing certain music videos. The industry—from rappers to label execs—was more than happy to hang the network out to dry while BET was out there alone fighting for their First Amendment rights. I never forgot that fact as I crafted the vision of the network moving forward. I listened to the shouts of those protestors *and* the silence of the industry to make my decision. Standards were loosening across the board, and BET was getting the blame for it. No more. If the network was going to be criticized, it would be because of a clear-eyed decision based on the company's values, not the whims of a constantly shifting industry. After decades of experience and more than a few wins, I was sure of my voice and unafraid to mold the network according to my own principles as a mother, a music lover, and a devotee to Black culture overall. Case in point: "bitch."

I hated the word "bitch." Everyone knew I didn't want to hear it on air. Our standard was no b-word and no n-word. But super producer Mara Brock Akil managed to change my mind. Acquiring Mara's football wives sitcom *The Game* for BET after the CW canceled it was the best programming decision I made in my entire three decades at the network. We had a scripted hit on our hands for the first time. And it wasn't just a BET record. Almost eight million viewers tuned in to watch the fourth season opener, making it the most watched sitcom premiere in cable TV history. We were shifting the narrative and doing it with programming that didn't exploit or talk down to its audience. Before *The Game* premiere, our most watched hour of programming was an exclusive interview between O. J. Simpson and *BET News* anchor Ed Gordon. That had Bob's hands all over it. I was so happy when that hour was no longer our yardstick.

So Mara was my golden child. When she pitched me *Being Mary Jane* about a successful TV anchor navigating work, family, friends, and lovers, I didn't wait long to give her the green light. "Let's do it," I told Mara right there in the conference room. The show became our highest-rated drama. Mara was always pushing the envelope.

On her first show, *Girlfriends*, the four lead characters called each other "bitch" a lot. For them it was a term of endearment. But it still sounded like nails on a chalkboard to me. Language was important. We tried to air reruns of HBO's *The Wire*, and it was disaster. There were so many curse words bleeped out of the dialogue that folks couldn't follow the plot. The show flopped on BET.

The head of the NAACP, Bruce Gordon, once asked me, "Why are you different than HBO?" Great question.

"HBO is a paid network. BET is basic cable. We've got a broader, more conservative audience, and some of them have an issue with the language," I said, further cementing our company's moral compass for myself as I laid it out for Bruce. Because BET was on basic cable, meaning anyone could flip past it at any time, we had to appeal to a large swath of the demographic, not a select few. We couldn't go too edgy and air something like *The Wire* just because it had Black lead characters. It wasn't for us. I learned a lesson from that. We're not HBO, and we didn't need to be. HBO was HBO. We had our own lane, and we needed to stay in it. Our viewers wanted to see themselves depicted authentically, but they also expected us to be better and do better. We were supposed to be a filter. And I took my job as steward very seriously. But I softened a bit as time passed.

"Mara really wants to say 'bitch' on page 23," one of her producers would tell me from their set in Atlanta, pleading to get the go-ahead. Again, I was not a fan of the word. Call me old school, but I would never call any of my friends "bitches"—even as a term of endearment. I realize some women have reclaimed it, but "bitch" still didn't sit right with me, especially considering how hip-hop had used it as a slur to degrade women for decades. BET didn't need to add to that pile of disrespect. And I know there are plenty of women in positions of power who are hyper-aware that their passion and competitive drive could someday get them labeled a bitch. That was never my fear. If anything, I needed to be more aggressive to combat my "nice lady" image. Long story short, the word was fraught with meaning, and I wasn't going to be lazy about when and where to allow it on the network I ran. Depending on the context, I would say yea or nay. But they knew to always ask me first. "Let me see the rough cut," I'd say before making the final decision. The first season was a major success. Mara, her husband and producing partner Salim, and the drama's star, Gabrielle Union, were on the cover of magazines, on talk shows, doing late night. This was what I knew BET could be—a real network with a real vision. I still had stars in my eyes when Mara's team came back with an ask after the second season that I'll never forget.

In the third season, Gabrielle's character, Mary Jane Paul, is recovering from a freak car crash caused after she inadvertently found out that her ex and her best friend had a sexy past. Oh, the drama. The accident leaves MJ's face, her bread and butter, disfigured, and during the season, she has to bounce back both physically and emotionally. God, I loved this show. In the scene where MJ finally returns triumphantly to her TV studio as if all the drama of her personal life was water under the bridge, she's hitting the hallways like a catwalk, totally feeling herself. It was a powerful moment, and Mara wanted to underscore it with a song that had 38 "bitches" in it.

"We counted, Ms. Lee," said her producer. "Mara feels strongly that this represents where MJ is and it's really important to the story line."

My first inclination was to say, "Heck no." But after I watched a clip of the scene, I could see where Mara was going with this. I didn't raise the question to my team or focus group the decision. I just sat with it for a day or two before giving Mara's team my answer. "Y'all can use it. *This* time," I said. Giving that okay was a milestone for me. There was zero backlash from the episode. Zero. No angry calls, emails, or tweets. The rebrand had done what it needed to do. Our audience trusted our intentions. Thirty-eight "bitches"? No problem. We had proven the point. We were different than the other networks doing Black content. We'd shown our audience that they could expect more from us, so I could loosen the reins a bit. No one came to march in front of my house the next morning. We'd turned a corner.

Our viewers no longer jumped at the chance to criticize our every move. Like the time Lil Wayne performed his song "Every Girl"—about having sex with all the women he knew—and his preteen daughter Reginae hopped onstage with her friends to dance around with her dad. "How could BET allow that?" The answer is we didn't. It was a live show, and there was nothing the producers could do about it. But we, and I, bore the brunt of it.

The absolute worst was the time one of our writers made a thoughtless joke about Beyoncé's daughter, Blue Ivy. In a segment for our flagship video show *106 & Park*, a guest host delivered a silly (but hurtful) punchline about what Blue Ivy was thinking while the little girl sat next to her famous parents during the MTV Video Music Awards. The backlash was immediate. The Beyhive does not play. I was furious when I heard about it.

"Stephen, how did this happen?"

"It was a freelance producer, Debra. I'm sorry."

"Well, she has to go," I told him. Stephen didn't argue. We had an unspoken rule at the network. Let's call it the Beyoncé rule. You don't say anything negative about Queen Bey. Her fan base was fierce and loyal—and BET was a part of that. Not to mention the fact that the network had watched her grow up into one of the most influential artists of the century. Yeah, there was no dissing her on our channels ever. We issued a formal apology, and that producer was fired.

MTV would have never gotten the pushback we did over that joke. But we weren't MTV. Our viewers expected us to be more than a network. We were expected to be a caretaker. Our marching orders were to protect the integrity of the community. When I took over, that became our major operating principle— and we'd traveled so far that now years later there could be a song with 38 "bitches" in it, and no one would bat an eye.

But that didn't mean we could sit back and relax. Competition was brewing. BET was doing so well that the other networks started to realize that Black programming worked. The battle was on. Nobody could touch us in the ratings, but each night of the week the other networks would do their "Black night." On Monday, it was VH1. Tuesdays BET aired its original programming. Bravo stepped into the ring on Wednesday, and on it went. But no one touched Tuesdays. That was ours. All the networks quietly picked other nights of the week because they didn't want to go head-to-head with *The Game* or *Being Mary Jane*. The competition wasn't letting up though, especially when Tyler Perry started churning out content for TBS, but we still won out. Our ratings proved that high-quality programming had become our calling card. Overall, we were still the number one network in Black households for years. But I still waited to get the numbers on Wednesday mornings to make sure no other network had knocked us off the winner's block. We lived and died by Nielsen ratings. Then Oprah's network, OWN, decided to air Tyler's new shows on Tuesday night, our night. It was a declaration of war.

Oprah is Oprah. But when the Oprah Winfrey Network launched in 2011, none of her shows were hits. So, following a familiar formula, OWN started to dip its toe into programming for Black audiences. We build it, and then they will come. We were watching from BET HQ to see how far OWN planned on going. Its wholesome reality show *Welcome to Sweetie Pie's* was doing well enough, but I wasn't worried. Then Oprah got her pal

Tyler Perry to jump ship from TBS, and that's when I knew. She was coming for us.

I'd just come back from a much-needed vacation when my phone started blowing up with missed calls and voicemails from the office.

"What's going on, Bobette?"

"Oprah called! Twice."

"Well, what does she want?"

"She wouldn't say, but she wants to talk to you right away, Debra."

I was still basking in some leftover vacation vibes, so I didn't call Oprah back until I got home a few hours later and had a chat with my ad sales team to see if they knew what Ms. Winfrey wanted. I had an inkling of what this could be about. If the head of a network called not once but twice, this had to be about money, which meant advertising. "Their sales team called wanting to buy some time slots on BET. We told them no." Got it. I thanked my head sales executive and dialed Oprah Winfrey's number. The two of us had a conversation that I wish I could frame.

"...my people are telling me there's a problem," delivered Oprah in that unmistakable anchor's alto of hers.

"Oprah, I have no idea what you're talking about," I began. "Wait, is this about the ads?"

"They're saying we have a problem."

"There's no problem. This is not a personal issue. But competitors do not sell one another ad time on their networks. That's just not how this works. ABC does not advertise on CBS, and vice versa." I couldn't believe I had to explain this to her.

"Well," said Oprah, "I don't think of myself as a *competitor*," she added, emphasizing the word.

"If you're not a competitor, then you're in the wrong business. TV is about who wins every night."

"Yeah, yeah, I know. I get that. I just think it's more important how you walk through this earth than winning," said Oprah in all seriousness.

"I'm out to win. I'm not going to hand my audience to you on a silver platter."

"I guess it's like when I first started my talk show in Chicago and Phil Donahue called me and said, 'I wish you good luck but not in my time slot.'"

"Exactly. It's kind of like that. But BET is a 24-hour network."

We ended that call on decent terms but didn't speak to each other for a while after that. I couldn't believe that *the* Oprah Winfrey was trying to convince me that she didn't want to win. The woman is a business. She wants to win all the time. And if it was true that she didn't "walk through life" with that mindset, well, good luck to her. I was in the TV business, and it mattered to me that I won.

Business is competition. Period. I was running a network, and OWN was our rival, whether its CEO saw it that way or not. The two of us being Black and female didn't change that fact. As it turns out, at the time, three Black women were running cable networks—me, Oprah, and Cathy Hughes. We held one another in high regard, but that admiration didn't slow down the ratings race. No matter who was asking, if the request wasn't good for my network, I wouldn't do it. Don't let hero worship stop you from doing your job. If I was so in awe of Oprah Winfrey (and trust I was in awe of her) that I would allow a competing network to purchase ads on my air, then I should've been fired. Earlier in my career I might have tried to compromise in some way. But not today.

What do you do when you feel like you're at the mountaintop of your career and staring down? Do you look for another summit, do you make camp up there and relax a bit, or do you climb down to help more people up? Those are the kinds of questions I couldn't ask myself until I'd been in the CEO position for 12 years. I felt comfortable there. Maybe too comfortable.

When Bob Bakish took over as CEO of Viacom, I started to see those familiar red flags that had popped up periodically throughout my career. But now, with decades under my belt, instead of swatting them away, I followed them.

Bakish was the fourth Viacom CEO to whom I reported since the media conglomerate acquired BET in 2001. For a while, our relationship with the company was ideal. Sumner Redstone had promised to never get involved in programming and to keep BET headquartered in Washington. He'd kept that promise for years, even though people (and by *people*, I mean our viewers and our own employees) were skeptical at first.

When news of the sale leaked, the entire senior staff was at an executive retreat in Aspen. Behind-the-scenes negotiations had been underway for months, but only Bob and I had been involved. We'd kept it quiet because we'd known what the next day's headlines would read: "BET Selling Out!" Or at least we thought we'd kept it quiet. A *Washington Post* reporter got wind of the deal and tracked Bob down in Aspen to confirm the details. The news spread like wildfire, and our entire staff at BET HQ was in panic mode while their leaders were thousands of miles away in a ski chalet. "I hear people are sobbing in the hallways," one senior executive informed me.

"That's it. Party's over," declared Bob. The dozen of us were on a plane within hours to comfort our staff. *Your jobs are safe. We're not going anywhere.* Still, folks felt stabbed in the back. As if Bob had betrayed them.

How could we sell to a white company? Weren't we special? Bob's line of defense was plain. How many Black-owned companies do you know with $3 billion? This was the path to BET's legacy. And before we even considered Viacom's offer, Bob made the company agree that it wouldn't change us. BET would remain BET. And it did—for a while. More than that, we were thriving under my leadership. But nothing stays the same forever. Corporate promises last only as long as the people who make them. When a new sheriff arrives in town, the changes can be swift.

They began when Bob Bakish started as Viacom's CEO.

Bakish had been at Viacom for years and in his role as CEO of MTV International, we were peers on Philippe's senior team. When we finally met after his appointment to CEO at Viacom HQ in Manhattan, I was slightly relieved. I was looking forward to him learning more about BET Networks. After some ice-breaking chitchat about the weather and our kids, Bakish said, "Tell me about your team." I was in the middle of going down the list of my senior executives when he interrupted with his view of the strengths and weaknesses of my team. Of course, I pushed back. Pulling together a core group of incredible senior managers hadn't been easy. It was a formula that was always shifting. But I knew how to add a pinch here and take away there. "I'm sorry, what?" He apparently had already made up his mind with information from who knows who. I left that meeting concerned about what our future together would look like. I was an old pro at handling leadership changes. By the time Bakish came along I'd already survived four or more corporate restructures. My strategy was always to keep my head down and do work that was both essential and undeniable. Our programming was good, our business development was sound, and, most importantly, ratings and ad sales were up. Done, done, and done. All the CEOs I'd worked with before respected what I had built. They understood the BET brand and knew we were different from MTV and VH1, our sister networks. Basically, they left me and BET alone. As soon as Bakish took over, one of the first things he did was set up half a dozen task forces to assess Viacom's corporate structure.

"Why do we have BET and VH1?" asked Bakish during a team meeting. *This is not going to go well*, I thought, before dusting off a spiel I hadn't had to give in years. He'd set up focus groups of employees whose purpose was to review the overall company, and there was a specific group focused solely on the question mark hanging over VH1 and BET. *Should we just merge?* We fought hard to make the point that our brands were separate even though we both had Black viewership and deep ties to the music industry. All Black people aren't the same. If Bakish didn't know what made BET unique *and* necessary, then we were not on the same page. The fact that this was even a question to ask was troubling to me. Then there came the meetings where Bakish had me and the head of VH1 and MTV duke it out over which channel would produce what kind of Black programming.

"Let BET do scripted. We've proven we can manage high-quality programming, and our audience really responds," I suggested in a meeting. "And VH1 can take unscripted. *Love and Hip Hop* and *Basketball Wives*. You all have that formula down." See what I was doing here? Trying to sneak my criticism in with a compliment. I always felt unscripted shows had to be over the top to create the drama that could easily be written in with scripted shows. That did not work well with BET audience. "But we can do scripted too. The musician biopics are such a hot market right now," said the young man who was running VH1 and MTV. Of course they wanted those series, especially the ones featuring Black artists. When done right, they were a ratings juggernaut.

"We know. We did *The New Edition Story*, remember?" I said.

"Jodeci would love to get on that," he countered.

"Great. We've already got a call in to them."

We went around and around like that for an hour. I hated having to fight this hard to prove a point that I'd proven years ago. I could do this and do it well. Nearing 64 years old, is this what I wanted my days to look like? Arguing with executives 20 years my junior about a Jodeci bio pic? Fighting for space we'd claimed and reclaimed? I think not. The writing was on the wall. And in the *New York Post*.

Less than six months after Bakish took over an article in the *Post* announced that my days at Viacom "were numbered." Oh, really, now?

"Is there something you want to tell me?" I asked Bakish over the phone. After reading the story several times, I had calmed myself down and dialed his direct line.

"There is zero ounce of truth to that *Post* story. Debra, you don't have anything to worry about," he assured me. I said okay and went back to doing my job, but a familiar alarm kept getting louder in the back of my mind. All the division heads at Viacom were fighting for leverage and more resources. The environment at the company at large was cutthroat and political, nothing like the supportive office culture I'd tried to nurture at BET since taking over. I tried to stay out of the corporate drama of who got to fly on which plane and who was invited to what business strategy meeting. I liked my job and felt I was living out my purpose of uplifting a culture I loved deeply. But the BS got harder to ignore.

The slope was getting slippery. While in the end Bakish sided with me that BET should take over scripted programming, the infighting continued. At this point, I had a reputation. BET was being lauded and getting recognition for the work we were doing. *The Game* premiered to 7.7 million viewers. *Being Mary Jane* was the hottest drama on basic cable. *The New Edition Story* held on to more than 2 million viewers every night for three consecutive nights. Lee Daniels even called me to ask who had directed the series. The next thing I knew, that same person was directing *Empire* on Fox. Imitation was the best form of flattery. But the competition inside the company was even more brutal. At upfronts that year, the annual presentation of new TV programming for advertisers, all my colleagues were doing more Black programming: Nickelodeon, VH1, MTV, and Comedy Central. That hadn't been the case even five years before. "Wow, their reels look a lot like ours," I told my PR person. It was hard enough to compete with other networks, but when it was your own people? Even some of my executives were cozying up to Viacom's brass in anticipation of a change at the top. Folks were out for themselves. We'd lost that "we're all in this together" magic of the earlier days at BET that made the late nights and breakneck pace worth it. When what we were doing felt urgent and revolutionary. Bob Johnson's old adage—"have fun and make money"—didn't ring true anymore. We were doing a lot of the latter, but for me, it just wasn't any fun anymore.

I didn't want to run the whole shebang one day. I wasn't jockeying for Bakish's position at Viacom. My autonomy was my freedom. I loved the body of work we'd created, the world we'd built at BET focusing on Black culture. Being CEO of Viacom would pluck me from the programming trenches I'd grown to love, pushing me further and further from the work I was actually passionate about. As far as I was concerned, my career would end at BET. So what did I want to do?

"Debra? Debra?" This was my lawyer talking. I'd asked him to lunch to discuss my options. I was under contract at Viacom but seriously considering my next move, and I needed his advice. So I unloaded all my work–life drama, complaining nonstop for a good 10 minutes about the infighting, the petty grievances, the programming challenges that I always said would be the final push. My lawyer asked the question I'd been asking myself lately: "So what do you want to do?" And I still wasn't quite ready with an answer.

He looked me in the eyes: "Debra, I hear you. In the media industry, every now and then, it's just your time to leave. You can stay and fight and raise a ruckus—or you can decide this is your time to leave." A light bulb went off. I didn't have to do a lot of deep soul searching. I didn't have to go back and forth for months on it. When it's your time, it's your time.

Let's do the numbers. I was 65. I'd been CEO for 13 years, COO for 10 years, and general counsel for nine before that. Most executives don't make it four or five years as CEO. It's like being in the NFL. I was an elder stateswoman. I loved what I was doing; every day was something new but also another fight. I'd been fighting so much during my career; it took a moment for me to realize when it was time to hang up my jersey.

"Give yourself some time," said my lawyer, "and then go talk to Bakish. Tell him you don't feel like you're on his team." I left that lunch feeling a lot lighter. Just the possibility of leaving BET gave my mood a boost.

Before I could backslide, another sign showed up. This time in the form of Ken Chenault, then the CEO of American Express and the third Black person to head a Fortune 500 company. I'd recognized

Ken at BET Honors one year because I don't think enough people knew that the company handing out those "Black cards" the hip-hop community kept going on about was run by a Black man.

"How are you doing?" asked Ken when the two of us bumped into each other at a party in the Hamptons. I was still in fight-or-flight mode but leaning heavily toward flight. But, no one save my lawyer knew what was going on.

"I'm doing okay, you?"

"I'm good. We should have lunch soon," he suggested. The next thing I knew I was in Ken's private executive dining room. After the niceties were out of the way, he asked about how things were at Viacom.

"It's funny because I've been thinking about my exit strategy. The hard thing is I've spent more than half my life at BET. Leaving feels almost wrong somehow, you know?"

"If you want to leave, you should leave," said Ken bluntly, delivering a hard truth that I desperately needed. That's when my eyes started misting over. The emotions hit me so hard I had to excuse myself. When I came back composed a few minutes later, Ken kept the gems coming.

"You know what your problem is, Debra? You have a founder's mentality. You feel like one of the founders of BET, but BET is not your company. You don't owe it anything. The company is in great shape. You've acquitted yourself well of your responsibility to BET and now it's time to focus on yourself. If you're ready to leave, then do it. Don't worry about what they do after. Those decisions aren't yours. It's not your company."

Ken's advice was a stab to the heart and a weight off my shoulders all at once. *It's not your company.* Wow. What a thought. So much of me *was* BET. I'd learned to trust myself, take risks, and tap into my power. I'd been creative, and I'd been strategic. I'd birthed my children. I'd made my fortune. I'd fought through harassment and toxicity. I'd changed the tires on the airplane while it was midflight, course-correcting a legacy brand to give it new life. I was a success. But it wasn't my company. I'd done enough. I couldn't be responsible for BET forever.

As a corporate leader, it's easy to get caught up in the story of your company. But that is not *your* story. Ken helped me see that. If I was a founder, my perspective would have been much different. In that frame of mind, the company's fortunes would 100 percent be my own. Founders get so wrapped up in their business that they think it can't survive without them. That can send you over the edge. And BET wasn't mine, no matter how long I'd been there and how connected to the people, the work, and the audience I was. It was freeing to see myself as a cog in a larger machine. I basically worked for Viacom, and now I was going to punch the clock for the last time. I'd made a lasting impact, there was no doubt about that. But I wasn't indispensable. I could leave.

Without Ken's final push, I might have spent more months on the fence. That's what network building can do—provide you with much-needed fresh perspective from someone who knows the direction you're headed. Often "network" is treated as a pejorative. But forming bonds outside your office is key to your overall career health. Ken was a business contact and a friend, but during that lunch in his office, Ken was a mentor. He took it upon himself to help me personally, and he didn't have to do that. Less than six months later he announced he was stepping down from AmEx after more than 17 years as CEO. He was asking himself the same questions he'd asked me. Now what?

I was finally ready to take my lawyer's advice and "go talk to Bakish."

Bakish was surprised when I delivered the news that it was time for me to go. "I thought you would stay a couple more years and give me time to find your successor," he said. He did have a point. I hadn't had time to groom a number two because I kept losing people on my team in the constant Viacom restructuring that would happen whenever a new CEO took over and started cutting costs and jobs. But like Ken said, this was their issue not mine. Not my company, not my problem. It was October, and I told Bakish I wanted to leave by the end of the year. Why drag this out? I knew a lot about the tragedy of long goodbyes. BET and I needed a swift, clean break. It'd be better for the both of us.

The board thought differently. They knew what my leaving might mean to our audience. My exit would mark an end of an era. I was one of the last executives at the company who had actually lived through its dynamic history. "Give us more time," they asked. I agreed to stay at BET until July.

By then I'd already moved to California. Viacom had shuttered BET's Washington headquarters, and the choice between Los Angeles or Manhattan was easy because my kids were in LA. Whether I recognized it or not, my transition had been in motion long before I walked into Bob Bakish's office that day to finally say the words "I'm leaving."

"How could you let this happen?" asked one of my top executives, a woman I had hired, through tears. News of my departure was making the rounds. "Does the board know? Why didn't you fight this?" She looked at me like I'd betrayed her. She reminded me of the women who'd cheered when Bob Johnson announced my appointment as COO. The women who gave me high fives in the hallway when I made it to CEO. They were so happy to see me—to see us—win. To them, me leaving was akin to me giving up. No one had a clue how hard I'd fought to stay and how much I'd sacrificed—my marriage, time with my kids, my own mental health—to lead BET. My fight was over. It was someone else's turn. I wasn't throwing in the towel. I was choosing a different ring altogether.

"The board knows," I told her. "We've agreed on a timeline. I'm receiving the lifetime achievement award at the BET Awards in June, and then that's it. BET is not my company, and it's time for me to walk away. I hope everything works out." In truth, I was feeling kind of guilty. I'd hired so many of the women walking the halls. Me leaving would be a huge change for them too. I was more than a little worried about how they'd fare under what regime would be put in place after I left. I had to trust that I'd taught them well. That I'd showed them what leading with your values looked like. That my example had given them a model to follow. Like when I told one EVP that she needed to sit at the head of the table when she ran meetings. "Oh, Debra. That doesn't really matter," she told me. But I wouldn't let it go. "Symbols matter. Maybe not to you, but they do to them," I said, nodding toward the men in the room. "You earned it. Take it." She never let anyone sit in her seat again. I'd exposed them to the Viacom brass and encouraged several to join corporate boards of other companies and find charitable opportunities outside of work. They saw how I did it and what was important to me. I'd set them up to be successful, passing on as much knowledge as I could on my way up and on my way out. It was their turn now.

It wasn't until around Christmas that year that I started feeling down. Seven more months? Is this what being a lame duck was like? I was in the office but not of the office. Decisions about programming I wouldn't be able to see to fruition felt less urgent. Hiring was frozen. The team was split between two coasts. While I was excited about my next chapter, this old one felt like a tether. Staring down more months in limbo was depressing. And here's the thing when you've climbed up the ladder that high: Few people know what it's like—the stress of your day-to-day and the weight of untangling yourself from that. Which is why Ken's advice was so necessary. On top of that, there were few women who knew what a transition this big would mean. Starting over at 65? Sure, it was freeing, but let's not forget that it was also terrifying. I was stewing in all those emotions when I decided to figure out what I could look forward to in the next 12 months.

The answer to that was easy: Leading Women Defined, my annual conference for the hundred most powerful Black women in media, politics, tech, education, entertainment, all of it. At that point I had been hosting it for a decade. It started when I took over as CEO, looked around, and realized there wasn't anything out there for us—women of color who were crushing it. Obama administration bigwigs Valerie Jarrett and Lisa Jackson spoke at our first gathering. Legendary civil rights activist Dorothy I. Height was there too in one of her last public appearances before her death. We raised awareness around mental health, raised money for Haiti, and then raised the roof all night on the dance floor. The women looked forward to it every year. I'd conceived it, planned it, and used my own Rolodex for the invite list.

Hillary Clinton was at Leading Women as a presidential candidate the night she won Super Tuesday. She spoke to the group and then immediately rushed backstage as the results were coming in. I stood beside her as she wrote her speech. It was one of those pinch-me moments. When Michele Obama showed up, I knew I had something special. This is how it happened: We were on Martha's Vineyard, as you do, and my good friend Sela Collins was telling the first lady of the United States about how great Leading Women was. "It's the best conference there is," she said. "You should come." Mrs. Obama was intrigued.

"Yeah, that does sounds interesting. Let me know about this year in DC," said Michele.

"Unfortunately, we just moved to Miami," I told her.

"I will get there," she said. And that was that.

Having something to look forward to—my continued board work, Leading Women Defined—made my last few months at BET easier. I felt like I was running toward a new purpose instead of leaving one behind. But before I could go, there was one last stage this former shy little girl from Greensboro had to conquer.

My driver, Trevor, was pissed. When we pulled up to the talent parking lot at the Microsoft Theater in Los Angeles for my last BET Awards, my regular spot—the CEO spot—was already taken.

"It's not right, Ms. Lee! They should've given you one more day," said Trevor from the front seat as I tried to collect my thoughts in the back. I'd known this day was coming for months, but my emotions were still running the gamut—happy, sad, nervous, exhausted.

"He can have it, Trevor. I'm leaving, remember?"

"It's just disrespectful!" he said before climbing out of the car.

"Don't worry about it," I said. "It's not a big deal." And the calm that washed over me was almost shocking. It wasn't a big deal. I was moving on and I was okay with that.

The walk up the red carpet was a happy blur. I know I told people I was honored to be receiving the Ultimate Icon award and that BET's legacy would continue. It wasn't until I got to the back-stage green room to get my hair and makeup touched up that the nerves creeped in. And LL Cool J was the main culprit. Like every living and breathing woman in the world, I had a little crush on LL, knowing full well he was happily married. My female exec-utives knew about the crush, so many times over the years, they asked LL to present me with various awards and do skits with me at the TV upfronts. They knew I'd always lose my cool around him, and they loved seeing me blush. So it was only fitting that he present my last award at BET that evening.

We exchanged some brief hellos, and that was it. He didn't say another word, and neither did I. We both knew we had to hold it together. While I was getting my blond curls fluffed, LL gave me a knowing look from his seat in the room as if to say, "I know this is hard on you, but job well done!" I nodded my head in a thank-you. For the next five minutes, we both sat in complete silence while getting prepped to go on air in front of millions.

"Ms. Lee?" said a producer in a headset. "They're ready for you."

I was on my way back to the front row during the commercial break when I spotted Jesse Collins, who had produced the BET Awards for years. Jesse and his crew knew me too well. Over the years, they'd comforted me backstage as my nerves got the better of me. "Breathe," he said before giving me a wink. They always let me know they had my back and would never let me fall. Seeing Jesse and his team helped center me as my insides were doing back flips. *Yes, I'm working with the best in the business, and yes, I got this.*

When LL called my name from the stage, I barely heard it. Quinn took my arm and guided me up the steps as I walked to the microphone, addressing the industry, my kids, my family, my friends, my team, and the more than 10 million fans watching at home and around the globe.

"Growing up I was a fan of beautiful Black brands like *Ebony* and Motown, so naturally I was excited 32 years ago to join a Black-owned company that created content specifically for a Black audience." I looked out and spotted Jamie Foxx, who'd hosted *Walk of Fame* all those years ago; Kendrick Lamar, whom my son once had sleeping on my couch in DC; Janelle Monae, whom I'd watched perform at the White House at one of the last big concerts BET hosted there during Obama's presidency. Keeping my voice from cracking was hard. Heck, standing upright was hard. Those five minutes at the mic were like *This Is Your Life* on steroids. Everything came crashing down on me as I read the teleprompter.

"Over my 32-year career at BET Networks—it's a long time—there are two things I never got tired of hearing. First, I grew up on BET, and second, my first industry job was at BET. I love that BET has been a place where we can see authentic images, celebrate our culture, and just be unapologetically Black. The power of Black culture is unmatched. It's beautiful. It's amazing. It's everything. It's us."

I'm not sure how I got through it all. I wanted to cry but knew I couldn't. I had to keep it together no matter what. I had learned how to do that over the years. "I'd like to also say something to all the little Black girls. I hope you look at my career as proof that you can be and do anything you want to do because you rock and don't let anyone ever tell you any different." After thanking my kids, I dropped the proverbial mic. My 32-year career at BET was over once I walked off that stage. It was a job well done, but that didn't mean that I was done. I was entering my passion phase and couldn't wait to see what came next.

LEGACY

My son Quinn once asked me if he'd ever gone through anything really traumatic in his life.

"I don't know, son, maybe me and your dad breaking up?"

"No, no, that wasn't that bad," he said.

"I'm not sure I can think of anything else," I said.

"I guess maybe I don't have any."

"That's good, Quinn. That's a good thing. Don't make any up."

I thought about that conversation a lot after Quinn died. He lit up every room he was in. He was the absolute coolest kid. Music was everything to him. A crowd of pulsating bodies moving to the beats he spun as a DJ was like a battery. When the pandemic first hit and life as we knew it disappeared, it was as if someone turned the music off. Losing him was unbearable for me, for Ava, for

Randy, for anyone who'd been touched by this incredible human being who wanted nothing more than to make people smile and dance. He was also a talented A&R guy who had a knack for finding exciting young music talent. The one thing that pulled us through the grief was his love—and the legacy he would leave for those that followed behind him.

I miss Quinn every single day. I love him unconditionally and he knows that. He loves me unconditionally and I know that. We were each other's biggest cheerleaders. I miss his advice on music, the latest trends in clothing, the hottest restaurants, and what shows and movies to watch. He was inclusive and loving to everyone he met. He makes us all proud.

If there is anything I wish I could've told my son it's that our difficulties don't define us. That trauma and hardship don't make us who we are. That we all either have been through it or are going through it. There is no shame or embarrassment about struggling. I have struggled. Despite what millions saw on those stages, the red carpets, the magazine covers, there was often something more painful playing out behind my smile or backstage. I want everyone to know that. That's why I wrote this book. To show that success and self-doubt are not mutually exclusive. That your highest highs can be followed by your lowest lows. And you are not alone. You don't have anything to be ashamed of.

And on the other side of the struggle—even if you can't see it, feel it, or imagine it—there is joy waiting for you. If there is anything I've learned in my career and life, it's that holding on can feel impossible, but I promise you, it's worth it.

ACKNOWLEDGMENTS

I would like to thank my parents for molding me into the woman I am today. Major Richard M. Lee, my father, taught me drive, grit, and the importance of education. He always told me I could do anything I wanted to do and placed no limits on me because of my gender. My mother, Delma L. Lee, taught me compassion, grace, and humility.

My attorney, Deneen Howell, did not flinch when I told her I wanted to write a book. Thank you for your publishing expertise and your friendship.

I would like to thank my collaborator, Helena Dryer Andrews. You made the writing process fun even in the midst of a pandemic. You helped me do it for the culture!!

I would like to thank my editor and publisher, Krishan Trotman, and her team at Legacy Lit and Hachette Book Group,

ACKNOWLEDGMENTS

Amina Iro, Carolyn Kurek, Tara Kennedy, Brian McClendon, Albert Lee, Melanie Schmidt, Melissa Mathlin, and Thomas Mis. Krishan understood the importance of my story and my hope that it would inspire young women and men. Thank you, Krishan, for your belief in me from day one. I would like to thank Vernon Jordan, who was the first person to suggest I write a book about my life and career.

Also, thanks to Michele Bourne, Thomas Motley, Sherri Blount, and Brickson Diamond, my crew. Thanks for listening to my stories throughout the years and offering support during good and bad times.

Finally, I would like to thank others who have supported me and inspired me over the years: Michelle Obama, Kamala Harris, Hillary Clinton, Ruth Simmons, Cicely Tyson, Gretta Lee, Ron Lee, Yolanda Caraway, Jeanine Liburd, Channing Johnson, Gabrielle Glore, Bobette Gilette, and Maia Barnett.

ABOUT THE AUTHOR

Debra L. Lee is a trailblazer. For thirteen years she served as the chairman and CEO of Black Entertainment Television, the leading provider of entertainment for the African American audience and consumers of Black culture globally. With a trendsetting career spanning over three decades, Lee is one of the most influential female voices in the entertainment industry.

During her tenure as CEO from 2005 to 2018, Lee helmed BET's reinvigorated approach to original authentic programming that led to hits such as *The Game, The New Edition Story, Being Mary Jane, The BET Awards, Black Girls Rock!, BET Honors,* and many more.

Named one of the *Hollywood Reporter*'s 100 Most Powerful Women in Entertainment and Billboard's Power 100, Lee's sizeable impact on the cable industry and corporate world writ large has been recognized again and again. She was inducted into the Broadcasting + Cable Hall of Fame, and the Advertising Hall of Fame.

In February 2017, she became the first woman to receive the Grammys' Salute to Industry Icons Award, in recognition of her major contributions to American music and culture.

Lee is the founder and chairman of the Leading Women Defined Foundation, an organization committed to uplifting and supporting Black female thought leaders.

In 2021, Lee launched the Monarchs Collective, a venture created to put more people of color on corporate boards and in executive leadership positions. Currently she serves as a director on the boards of Warner Bros. Discovery, Burberry Group Plc., Marriott International, and Procter & Gamble. She previously served as a director of AT&T; WGL Holdings, Inc.; Twitter, Inc.; Eastman Kodak Company; and Revlon, Inc.

Lee earned her juris doctorate at Harvard Law School, while simultaneously earning a master's degree in public policy from the John F. Kennedy School of Government. She graduated from Brown University with a bachelor's degree in political science with an emphasis in Asian politics. In 2014, Brown University awarded Lee with a doctor of humane letters.

I am Debra Lee
MCN B Lee   **31659061799892**

Lee, Debra.
EAST BATON ROUGE LIBRARY

DUE DATE	MCN	03/23	29.00

MAIN

DISCARD